Hear the Rush
of Angel Wings

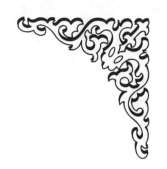

Hear the Rush
of Angel Wings

Joel and Jane French

New Leaf Press

First printing: October 1996

ISBN: 0-89221-329-9
Library of Congress Number: 96-69684

Cover illustration : Viv Eisner-Hess
Cover design: Left Coast Design, Inc., Portland, Oregon

Preface

All of the stories in this book are about people who have had angelic encounters. No fictional names are used. In the case of historical accounts of angels, every effort has been made to trace the story to its original documented source.

The mystery, purposes, and pursuits of angels are also fully explored. No stone is left unturned. Many people have been interviewed, but only the most valid experiences have been included. All should be intrigued by the thrilling true stories selected, from the most famous people of yesterday to the most famous of today. Young people should especially enjoy the stories of angels and children.

Many of the people interviewed have expressed the belief that they have had an angel watch over them. This book explores why many find comfort in picturing a beautiful guardian angel walking beside them, shielding them from danger, keeping them from harm's way, and guiding their steps and lives in the right direction.

Contents

Chapter 1

A Boy, a Snake, and an Angel

The boy and his dog shuffled through the lonesome landscape of dry brush near their isolated home in southwestern Florida. It was a mild, breezy February afternoon. Mark Durrance, 12, had finished Sunday dinner with his family and gone out with his BB gun to plunk at small animals.

Mark was handsome, with blond hair and bright blue eyes. He felt at ease in this remote country, surrounded by vast, open land.

With him this afternoon was Bobo, a medium-sized brindled mutt with a square, friendly face. These two happy wanderers were in rough land just right for boys and dogs . . . and venomous snakes.

As Mark and Bobo were heading home, the boy spotted a bird in a cabbage palm. With his eyes fixed on the bird, he leaped over a ditch. He landed on something that seemed to roll under the pressure of his right foot. Instantly Mark felt an explosion of pain. At first it was a numbing crush like an ax being slammed down on his foot. Then a searing jolt of furious heat savaged his lower leg. His BB gun flew from his hands as he looked down.

The massive head of an Eastern diamondback rattlesnake was plastered across his foot. Its heavily muscled jaw opened across the top of Mark's shoe in a ferocious grip. The fangs had pierced the leather and become embedded just in front of the anklebone. Scorched with pain, the boy stared down at the snake as it seemed to gnaw slowly and deliberately on his foot.

Then Mark was aware of his dog's loud snarling and snapping at the snake. Bobo kept darting in and nipping — 10 or 15 times — but the snake wouldn't let go. Then Bobo pounced and tore into the snake's head, and blood flew.

At that instant, Mark felt the serpent release its grip. He jerked his leg away, and the snake slithered off into the bushes.

Mark was 150 yards from his house. The breeze rustling through the palm leaves would obscure any cries for help. He must not panic, Mark told himself. His parents had taught him that the faster a person's blood flows, the faster the poison reaches the heart. Then Mark realized that he couldn't even move. The pain was overpowering. He felt weak all over, and everything started to get fuzzy.

Though Mark did not know it, the rattlesnake's fangs had injected a massive amount of venom directly into a vein. The poison was racing through his body, launching multiple attacks upon his respiratory system, his heart, and his body's ability to clot blood. It would take a miracle for the boy to cover 150 yards over rough terrain and then mount the steps to his door.

Bobby Durrance was pruning the bushes in his front yard when his oldest son, Buddy, came screaming; "Daddy! Mark's been snake bit!" A compact, muscular man who for a dozen years had worked in the oil fields, Bobby raced for the house and found Mark on the living room floor, unconscious, his mother Debbie beside him.

The boy smelled of the musky odor the Durrances had noticed when their animals had been struck by rattlesnakes. The only words Mark uttered had come calmly and peacefully from his lips as he walked through the door: "I've been rattlesnake bit." Then he fell to the floor unconscious, violent convulsions racking his body.

Debbie tore at Mark's shoes and uncovered an ugly, purple mound that looked to be grapefruit-size on his right foot. Without a telephone, Debbie and Bobby knew they had to drive for help. They twisted a tourniquet around Mark's leg. Then, with their son in their arms, they ran to their pickup truck and took off at top speed for the health clinic 17 miles away.

"Mark was completely limp," says Debbie. "I had him cradled in my arms. I kept his nose against my face, and his breathing was getting fainter and fainter. The only thing I could do was pray." Reaching into her own childhood for words her mother had promised would always bring strength, she repeated the 23rd Psalm.

Yea, though I walk through the valley of the shadow of death, I will fear no evil: for Thou art with me.

Bobby drove fast, hogging the road, passing cars, racing for his son's life. A mile short of the clinic, the truck began to sputter. A gauge showed that the motor was overheating. Then the engine cut off completely, and the truck rolled to a stop, still in the road.

Bobby jumped out and frantically waved his arms. Drivers swerved around him. Bobby ran back to the truck and took Mark from Debbie's arms. He carried him to the middle of the road and held the boy's limp, almost breathless body up in the air like a flag.

One car slammed on its brakes. The driver, a Haitian farm worker, spoke no English, but he understood. He urged Debbie and her unconscious son into his car and followed Debbie's hand-motion directions to the clinic.

The staff there tried to stabilize the boy, but he needed more help than they could give. They started intravenous fluids, began artificial respiration, and sent Mark by ambulance to the nearest hospital — ten miles away in Naples.

Dr. Michael Nycum, a general surgeon, was at home washing his boat when he got word of the emergency. He sped to the hospital's emergency room and was waiting as the ambulance pulled in. "By then, the boy had quit breathing on his own," says Nycum. "He was practically dead."

Over the next eight hours, four doctors and a battery of nurses worked ceaselessly over Mark. "His whole cardiovascular system was on the brink of collapse," says Dr. Nycum. "And then his kidneys shut down." The venom prevented Mark's blood from clotting — causing internal hemorrhaging. All of this was complicated by the failure of his respiratory system. "For the first 12 to 14 hours, the only thing the little guy had going for him was his heart, and that was under tremendous stress," says Dr. Nycum.

Every aspect of Mark's body was besieged by the venom, which in such quantity has a direct toxic effect on blood as well as tissues. It kills cells. The doctors gave Mark doses of antivenin, a serum derived from the blood of horses injected with snake venom. Still, medically speaking, there was no realistic chance of saving the boy's life.

"Usually, in such a drastic case, we begin to see some turnaround within a couple of hours, or we lose the battle," says Dr. Nycum. "We didn't see this with Mark. He was as critical after eight hours as he was when we first saw him."

By Monday morning, Mark had begun to stabilize. His blood pressure improved slightly. There were signs of kidney activity. But he remained in a coma.

For Debbie and Bobby the most horrifying aspect was the blood that seeped steadily from Mark's ears, mouth, and eyes. And then there was the hideous swelling of every part of his body. His hands were three times normal size. He appeared to have no neck. "His eyes were swollen so tight that all we could see were the ends of eyelashes along the slits of his eyes," Debbie remembers. "And blood seeped from the slits." Before it was over, he was given 18 pints of blood.

On Tuesday, the doctors became concerned that the swelling in Mark's right leg might shut down the blood flow to his foot, forcing the amputation of his lower leg. Jagged incisions were made along his leg so the swollen tissue could expand-thus relieving the pressure on the blood vessels.

Debbie never left the hospital. She sat for hours, praying over her son and comforting him: "He may have been in a coma, but I believed he might hear my words to him and to God."

On the third day, Mark began to regain consciousness; on the fourth, he was removed from the respirator. During the first few moments, doctors listened intently as Mark spoke to his parents. Though his voice was scratchy, he told with striking clarity about how he had jumped the ditch and landed on the rattlesnake. Laughter mingled with tears when Mark said he hoped his father was not angry with him for being so careless. To the doctors, this clarity was a sign that Mark's brain had not been damaged.

The doctors and nurses left the bedside. Only the boy's parents remained.

Debbie rubbed her son's swollen brow and gently held his bloated hand. It was during these moments, when Mark and his parents were alone in this loving cocoon of humble thanksgiving, that the boy told them of an extraordinary event that took place in the desolate field — an occurrence that harks to the Old Testament's stirring accounts of men and angels.

Mark explained with perfect composure about a white-robed figure who appeared just when he knew that he could not walk the distance to the house. The figure took him in his arms and carried him across the field and up the steps.

"I know it was God," Mark said. "He had a deep voice. I felt calm. He picked me up and carried me all the way. He told me that I was going to be sick, but not to worry, that I would make it. Then He went up into the sky. The last thing I remember was opening the door to our house."

Not a particularly religious boy, Mark told his story with a seriousness that deeply impressed his family. Knowing the valley of death through which their son had just passed, Bobby and Debbie Durrance believed every word.

As Mark improved, he and his father discussed the boy's experience. They figured that when Mark's right foot came down on the snake's midsection, the rattler whipped back and sank its fangs into his foot. While rattlers normally pull back quickly after a defensive strike, it is possible that the snake's fangs were caught in the leather of Mark's shoe and that the chewing motion was actually the snake's effort to loosen its grip. That motion may have pumped an extraordinary amount of venom into the boy's foot. On the basis of the width of the fang marks — more than 1-1/2 inches after the swelling had subsided — and other factors, experts estimate that the snake was at least six feet in length.

As for what took place after that, it is beyond any natural explanation. What Mark says happened can never be proved, but such things never lend themselves to proof. Somehow, the boy made it 150 yards over rough terrain and up 13 steps and then opened the door to his house.

Says Dr. Nycum: "From a medical standpoint, I don't know how he could have done it." But Mark knows with absolute certainty.

Mark Durrance is a quiet boy with a direct and attentive gaze. He possesses a calmness that Dr. Nycum describes as "stoic." "No single medical procedure brought him around," says Dr. Nycum, "only the ceaseless energy of many people. He's a tough little guy, and he comes from strong people," concludes Nycum. "What brought him through was a lot of hard work and a lot of praying."

Numerous skin-grafting operations await Mark, as doctors work to rebuild the tissue on his leg and foot. However, Dr. Nycum believes that Mark will suffer no lasting disability.

Mark, moreover, is eager to return to the back country with Bobo and his BB gun. When he grows up, he hopes to be a farmer, so he can work on the land he loves.

Mark's parents are deeply thankful for the doctors and nurses. They also wonder about the kindly Haitian farm worker. "I don't know what would have happened without that man," says Debbie. "By the time I went to thank him, he was gone. We never knew his name."

Mark understands that he goes forward in this life with a very special blessing — the sure knowledge that as a child he was held in the hands of God.[1]

[1] Henry Hurt, "A Boy, a Snake, and an Angel," *Readers Digest*, Pleasantville, NY 10570, August 1988 issue. Used with permission.

Chapter 2

Angels Visit General George Washington

The last time I ever saw Anthony Sherman was on the Fourth of July, 1859, in Independence Square. He was then 99 years old, his dimming eyes rekindled as he gazed upon Independence Hall, which he had come to visit once more. The following is his story.

I want to tell you an incident of Washington's life — one which no one else alive knows of except myself; and which, if you live, you will before long see verified.

Washington — a Man of Prayer

From the opening of the Revolution, we experienced all phases of fortune, good and ill. The darkest period we ever had, I think, was when Washington, after several reverses, retreated to Valley Forge, where he resolved to pass the winter of 1777. Ah! I often saw the tears coursing down our dear commander's careworn cheeks, as he conversed with a confidential officer about the condition of his soldiers. You have doubtless heard the story of Washington's going to the thicket to pray. Well, he also used to pray to God in secret for aid and comfort.

A Vision of Future Events

One day, I remember well, the chilly winds whispered through the leafless trees. Though the sky was cloudless and the sun shone brightly, he remained alone in his quarters nearly all afternoon. When he came out, I noticed that his face was a shade paler than usual, and there seemed to be something on his mind of more than ordinary importance. Returning just after dusk, he dispatched an orderly to the quarters of the officer I mentioned who was in attendance at the time. After a preliminary conversation of about half an hour, Washington, gazing upon his companion with that strange look of dignity that he alone could command, said to the latter: "I do not know whether it is due to the anxiety of my mind, or what, but this afternoon, as I was preparing a dispatch, something seemed to disturb me. Looking up, I beheld, standing opposite me, a singularly beautiful being. So astonished was I, for I had given strict orders not to be disturbed, that it was some moments before I found language to inquire the cause of the visit. A second, a third, and even a fourth time did I repeat my question, but received no answer from my mysterious visitor, except a slight raising of the eyes. By the time I felt strange sensations spreading through me, and I would have risen, but the riveted gaze of the being before me rendered volition impossible. I assayed once more to speak, but my tongue had become useless, as though it had become paralyzed. A new influence, mysterious, potent, irresistible, took possession. All I could do was to gaze steadily, vacantly, at my unknown visitor. Gradually the surrounding atmosphere seemed to become filled with sensations, and grew luminous. Everything about me seemed to rarefy, including the mysterious visitor.

"I began to feel as one dying, or rather to experience the sensations which I have sometimes imagined accompany dissolution. I did not think, I did not reason, I did not move; all were alike impossible. I was only conscience of gazing fixedly, vacantly at my companion."

Settlement and Expansion of the United States

"Presently I heard a voice saying, 'Son of the Republic, look and learn,' while at the same time my visitor extended an arm eastwardly. I now beheld a heavy vapor at some distance rising fold upon fold. This gradually dissipated, and I looked out upon a strange scene. Before me lay spread out in one vast plain all the countries of the world — Europe, Asia, Africa, and America. I saw rolling and tossing between Europe and America the billows of the Atlantic, and between Asia and America lay the Pacific.

" 'Son of the Republic,' said the same mysterious voice as before, 'look and learn.' At that moment I beheld a dark, shadowy being as an angel standing, or rather floating, in mid-air between Europe and America. Dipping water out of the ocean in the hollow of his hand, he cast some on Europe. Immediately a cloud raised from these countries, and joined in mid-ocean. For a while it remained stationary, and then moved slowly westward until it enveloped America in its murky folds. Sharp flashes of lightning gleamed through it at intervals, and I heard the smothered groans and cries of the American people. A second time the angel dipped water from the ocean and sprinkled it out as before. The dark cloud was then drawn back to the ocean, in whose billows it sank from view.

"A third time I heard the mysterious voice saying, 'Son of the Republic, look and learn.' I cast my eyes upon America and beheld villages and towns and cities spring up one after another until the whole land from the Atlantic to the Pacific was dotted with them. Again I heard the mysterious voice say, 'Son of the Republic, the end of the century cometh; look and learn.'

The Civil War Anticipated

"And this time the dark, shadowy angel turned his face southward, and from Africa I saw an ill-omened specter approach our land. It flitted slowly over every town and city of the latter. The inhabitants presently set themselves in battle against each other. As I continued looking, I saw a bright angel, on whose brow rested a crown of light on which was traced the word 'Union,' bearing the American flag, which he placed between the divided nation. He said, 'Remember, ye are brethren.' Instantly the inhabitants, casting down their weapons, became friends once more, and united around the national standard.

America to Be Invaded by Foreign Foes

"Again I heard the mysterious voice saying, 'Son of the Republic, look and learn.' At this the dark, shadowy angel placed a trumpet to his lips and blew three distinct blasts; and taking water from the ocean, he sprinkled it on Europe, Asia, and Africa. Then my eyes beheld a fearful scene. From each of these countries arose thick black clouds that were soon joined into one; and throughout this mass there gleamed a dark red light by which I saw hordes of armed men, who, moving with the cloud, marched by land and sailed by sea to America, which country was enveloped in the volume of cloud. And I dimly saw these vast armies devastate the whole country and burn the villages, towns, and cities that I had beheld springing up.

"As my ears listened to the thundering of the cannon, the slashing of swords, and the shouts and cries of millions in mortal combat, I again heard the mysterious voice saying, 'Son of the Republic, look and learn.' When the voice had ceased, the dark angel placed his trumpet once more to his mouth and blew a long and fearful blast.

Our Country Emerges the Victor

"Instantly a light as of a thousand suns shown down from above me, and pierced and broke into fragments the dark cloud which enveloped America. At the same moment the angel upon whose head still shown the word 'Union' and who bore our national flag in one hand and a sword in the other descended from the heavens attended by legions of white spirits. These immediately joined the inhabitants of America, who I perceived were well-nigh overcome, but who, immediately taking courage again, closed up their broken ranks and renewed the battle. Again, amid the fearful noise of the conflict I heard the mysterious voice saying, 'Son of the Republic, look and learn.' As the voice ceased, the shadowy angel for the last time dipped water from the ocean and sprinkled it upon America. Instantly the dark cloud rolled back, together with the armies it had brought, leaving the inhabitants of the land victorious.

A Period of Reconstruction

"Then once more, I beheld the villages, towns, and cities springing up where I'd seen them before, while the bright angel, planting the azure standard he had brought in the midst of them, cried with a loud voice: 'While the stars remain, and the heavens send down dew upon the earth, so long shall the Union last.' And taking from his brow the crown on which blazoned the word 'Union,' he placed it upon the standard while the people, kneeling down, said 'Amen.'

Divine Intervention

"The scene instantly began to fade and dissolve and I, at last, saw nothing but the rising, curling vapor I had at first beheld. This also disappeared, and I found myself once more gazing upon the mysterious visitor, who in the same voice I had heard before said, 'Son of the Republic, what you have seen is thus interpreted. Three great perils will come upon the Republic. The most fearful is the third [The help against the third peril comes in the shape of divine assistance], passing which the whole world united shall not prevail against her. Let every child of the Republic learn to live for his God, his land, and his union.' With these words the vision vanished, and I started from my seat and felt that I had seen a vision wherein had been shown me the birth, the progress, and the destiny of the United States."

"Such, my friends," said the venerable narrator, "were the words I heard from Washington's own lips, and America will do well to profit by them."[1]

---

[1] "George Washington's Vision," Osterhus Publishing House, 4500 W. Broadway, Minneapolis, MN 55422. Used with permission.

Chapter 3

An Angel Saves the Union During the Civil War

In the previous chapter we have read the story of General George Washington's vision. During that terrible winter of 1777 and '78, God spoke to the great general who later became our first president and showed him the entire future of the United States of America. He showed him the victory that would be won at the cost of many lives, the birth of the Union. He also was permitted to see the growth and development of the greatest nation on the face of the earth, its mighty cities and progress.

Closely related to Washington's vision, but not as well-known, is a vision which was given to General George B. McClellan, one of the generals who took part in the second peril to hit America (the Civil War).

The only source which is known to have an account of this vision is the *Evening Courier* of Portland, Maine, for March 8, 1862. It carries a lengthy account of a vision reported to be in McClellan's own words. The General was alive at the time and could have repudiated the account and demanded an immediate retraction if it had been false.

General McClellan is not as well-known as other military leaders in America. But he did serve his country well and was responsible for preserving our Union and was undoubtedly divinely assisted in this undertaking.

General McClellan had gone to Washington, DC, to take over the command of the United States Army. This being the third day of his arrival, he was working until two o'clock in the night checking the reports of scouts and studying his maps.

Being overcome with exhaustion and work, he leaned his head on his arms on the table and fell asleep.

About ten minutes later, the locked door was opened suddenly and someone entered and walked right up to him, and in a voice of authority said, "General McClellan, do you sleep at your post? Rouse you, or ere it can be prevented, the foe will be in Washington!"

The general then gave some details of his strange experience which followed. He told how he felt himself suspended in infinite space. Above him he heard a voice which startled him. He could not tell whether he was awake or asleep. The walls of the room, with its furniture and other objects, were no longer visible; but the maps covering the table were still before him. Then he found himself gazing upon a "living map" of America which extended from the Mississippi River to the Atlantic Ocean. The General was unable to identify the being standing next to him, except that it had the appearance of a man.

Then he looked at the mysterious map before him and was amazed to see the movements of the various troops; and as he watched, he realized he was seeing the complete picture of the enemy's lines and distribution of their forces. Being greatly elated, he felt he now knew what strategy to use to end the war speedily and victoriously.

But then his elation gave way to great apprehension because, on this moving map, he saw the enemy's soldiers moving to the very position he had intended to occupy in a few days. He then knew that the enemy was aware of his plan of attack.

Then the voice spoke again, "General McClellan, you have been betrayed. And had God not willed otherwise, ere the sun of tomorrow had set, the Confederate flag would have flown above the Capital and your own grave. But note what you see. Your time is short!"

Noting the movement of the troops on the "living map," he took his pencil and transferred their position to the paper map on his desk. Then McClellan was aware of the figure near him becoming luminous with light and glory. Raising his view, he looked into the face of George Washington!

Sublime and dignified, our first president looked upon the bewildered general and spoke the following. "General McClellan, while yet in the flesh I beheld the birth of the American Republic. It was indeed a hard and bloody one, but God's blessing was upon the nation and, therefore, through this, her first great struggle for existence, He sustained her and brought her out triumphantly with His mighty hand. A century has not passed since then, and yet the child Republic has taken her position as peer with nations whose pages of history extend for ages into the past. She has since those dark days, by the favor of God, greatly prospered. But now, by very reason of this prosperity, she has been brought to her second great struggle. This is by far the most perilous ordeal she has had to endure, passing as she is from childhood to open maturity. She is now being called upon to accomplish that vast result, self-conquest: to learn that important lesson of self-control, self-rule, which in the future will place her in the van of power and civilization.

"But her vision will not then be finished; for ERE ANOTHER CENTURY shall have gone by, the oppressors of the whole earth, hating and envying her exaltation, shall join themselves together and raise up their hands against her high calling they shall surely be discomfited, and then shall be ended her THIRD and last great struggle for existence. Thenceforth shall the Republic go on, increasing in power and goodness until her borders shall end only in the remotest corners of the earth, and the whole earth be blessed by her. Let her in her prosperity, however, remember the Lord her God, and let her trust be always in Him and she shall never be confounded."

After this, the heavenly visitor who appeared to be Washington raised his hand over General McClellan's head in blessing. A peal of thunder which rumbled through space awakened McClellan with a start, and he found himself in his room with his maps spread out before him on the table as they had been before he had dozed off.

As he looked upon the maps, he noticed a difference, for they were covered with marks, signs, and figures which he had made during the time he thought he had been sleeping. He stood up and started walking around the room to prove to himself that he was really awake and that he was seeing "straight." Then, taking another look at the maps, he found the markings still there.

Realizing this experience was divinely given, he ordered his horse saddled and went from camp to camp, ordering changes to be made which were necessary to frustrate the enemy's planned offensive. The strategy was successful and prevented the city of Washington from being captured. The Confederate Army, at that time, was so close to the capital that Abraham Lincoln, sitting in the White House, could hear the roar of the Confederate artillery.

Thus the Union was saved, and in the recorded story General McClellan concludes his account of his vision with these words: "The future is too vast for our comprehension; we are all children of the present. When peace shall again have folded her bright wings and settled upon our land, the strange, unearthly map which was marked that night by a supernatural hand shall be preserved among American archives, as a precious reminder to the American nation what they owe to God for His intervention in the second great struggle for existence. Verily, the works of God are above the understanding of man!"

* * * * *

I have no difficulty in accepting the validity of this dramatic account. I know that Moses and Elijah appeared in a glorified state to Peter, James, and John as they were with Jesus in the Mount of Transfiguration. God is able, in the same way, to speak to those whom He has placed in important places of leadership and give them direct guidance concerning their appointed task. Remember that those two Old Testament saints Moses and Elijah, spoke with Jesus about His coming death, thus preparing Him to go through it (Luke 9:31). The apostle Paul also had a vision of "a man of Macedonia" calling for him to come and help them (Acts 16:9-12). And John received the revelation of the Book of Revelation through a heavenly messenger who told John that he was a prophet in glorified form (Rev. 22:9). Why are we so ready to attribute the miraculous visitations of God to a satanic source? There is only a veil between the seen and the unseen world. Paul tells us that we are "compassed about with a great cloud of witnesses" (Heb. 12:1). Many translations render it "we are surrounded by a company of witnesses."

Praise God! America is not alone in this great peril. All the nations of the world may turn their backs upon us. They may leave our soldier boys to die on the battlefields alone, they may betray us in the midst of the battle; but if we ourselves will remain a holy nation, fulfilling the destiny which God has planned for us, then God will fight our battles and we will see the glory of the Lord as He cometh with ten thousand saints to execute judgment upon all (Jude 1:14).

[1] "An Angel Saves the Union," newsletter, End-Time Handmaidens, Inc., P.O. Box 447, Jasper, AR 72641. Used with permission.

Chapter 4

I Heard an Angel Call My Name

The rhythmic hum of the chopper engine and the constant echo of the popping blades might put a farm boy to sleep on a lazy Sunday afternoon at just about any place other than the jungles of South Vietnam. Dwight Franklin Fields and Floyd Dallas were both navy seamen with the special SEAL attachment from the aircraft carrier *America*, and were en route to enemy territory as forward observers. Only a few feet below them, the thick, dense jungle growth swayed rhythmically to the downward wind pressure of the chopper blades.

Having completed all necessary preparations for this mission, such as taping all loose articles which might make noise and alert the enemy as they moved quietly through the jungle to within a hundred yards of the enemy camp, they could now relax. Within a few minutes the chopper would drop them near the ground so they could begin their mission. They would be on their own in the jungle for the next eight days.

Dwight let his thoughts drift back to his early childhood on a dairy farm in Dexter, Missouri. A much more pleasant time in his life, he thought, as he remembered the wonderful meals his grandma cooked for him. "Frankie, Frankie, come quickly now. It's time to eat, Sonny Boy," she would call to bring him from his place of play. He smiled now as he remembered the wonderfully pleasant aroma of farm-grown bacon and eggs frying on a lazy spring morning in the beautiful Missouri countryside.

He wondered now why Grandma had always called him Frankie. No one else had ever called him by anything other than his real name. But Grandma insisted that little Sonny Boy was Frankie, not Dwight or Franklin. Maybe it was because he was her only grandson for several years and was always special to her. After all, she had raised him for the first several years of his life, as his parents had been busy day and night with their dairy farm.

And even though he was 20 years old, he still missed his grandma terribly at times. Only two years before, when he was 18 and fresh out of high school, she had hugged and kissed him goodbye as he left for the navy.

"Now take care of yourself, Frankie," she had called to him as he turned to wave back. "Remember, I'll be praying for you."

And as he thought about it now, he knew she was still praying for him. Although he had not seen her in a long time, he corresponded with her often by mail, and eagerly anticipated her encouraging letters.

The chopper made a sharp turn and then dropped straight down. Dwight's pleasant thoughts were abruptly interrupted as he jerked his complete attention to the task at hand. He and Dallas quickly made sure they had all their equipment and then jumped from the chopper, Dwight first, followed by Dallas. A sharp scream ricocheted above the swish of the chopper blades as Dallas hit the ground rolling. Unaware of a problem, the crew and the chopper quickly lifted above the dense jungle growth and disappeared.

A consuming feeling of loneliness and fear momentarily reached out and gripped Dwight. He shook it off as rigid training had taught him to do.

Dallas rolled on the ground as Dwight bent over him. Dallas's ring had caught in the chopper as he jumped and his finger had been completely severed from his hand. Dwight grabbed up Dallas to help him move quickly away from the drop site. Any enemy lurking nearby would easily locate them from the sound of the chopper as it lifted and moved away.

When they were well away from the drop site, Dwight centered his attention on Dallas's profusely bleeding hand. They made a pack out of mud and cigarette paper to stop the bleeding. That was about all they could do until medical help was available, as they were traveling light for their mission and had no medication with them.

Their job as forward observers was to move quietly, American Indian fashion, to within 50 or 100 yards of the enemy camp without being seen, so that they could radio back the enemy's exact position to artillery men located about eight miles to the south. The artillery unit would fire the big guns for a few minutes and then the forward observers would radio back any necessary corrections. Corrections made, the artillery unit would literally pound the enemy into the ground.

While the enemy was preoccupied with dodging heavy artillery fire, it was the job of the forward observers to gather up their equipment and escape from the immediate area as quickly as possible. They were to maintain complete radio silence for at least eight days and then, when a safe distance away, radio their position so that a chopper could pick them up. This was a good plan that had worked for Dwight and Dallas many times before with no problems. But never before had Dallas lost a finger and been forced to work under such horrendous pain.

As Navy SEALS they had been trained to work under near impossible conditions. They moved, without thought of turning back, quietly and quickly toward the enemy encampment. When they were within a hundred yards of the enemy they set up their equipment and began to calculate the coordinates for artillery fire. It was Dallas's job to operate the radio, and this he prepared to do without hesitation, even though the pain was almost unbearable and his hand had by now swelled to the size of a cantaloupe.

Dallas hurriedly radioed in the coordinates as Dwight gave them to him. All they had to do now was wait a few minutes for the firing to begin, radio in any corrections, and move quickly out of harm's way.

Within what seemed only a few seconds they found themselves at the wrong end of a firing range. They were being hit by friendly fire as trees came crashing down around them and their equipment was hit and demolished.

It took only a split second for them to realize what was happening as they made a dead run out of the target area and away from the enemy camp. In his numbness and dizziness from the severe pain, Dallas had called in their position rather than the enemy's position. Artillery fire had been directed at them full force. Fortunately, the procedure was to fire for only a few minutes and then cease firing until corrections were radioed in.

Since no corrections would be called in as the radio was lost, the artillery unit would know something was wrong and would not fire again. The observers had escaped the big guns, but still a greater problem loomed ahead. The enemy would know the artillery observers were near and would be out in full force hunting them down to prevent further artillery bombardment.

Dwight and Dallas ran for their lives throughout the rest of the night. At daybreak they slipped into a swamp to rest and carefully considered their plight. They were completely and hopelessly lost with only a knife, one canteen of water, and one rifle between the two of them. All other equipment, along with all their food and water, was either destroyed or left behind in their flight out of the artillery fire.

Dallas was almost delirious with pain. Dwight decided that the best plan was for them to move only at night through the swamps, avoid all villages because some of the enemy was sure to be in the villages, and to move in an easterly direction at all times. The enemy was north, so they could not move in that direction. If they went east they would sooner or later run into the ocean and perhaps an American ship could be signaled for help.

Their biggest fear was booby traps hidden along the trails. Many of their comrades had escaped enemy fire only to die a torturous death in some crudely made booby trap hidden in some completely unsuspecting place. Even the Viet Cong would seldom go into the swamps to set booby traps.

They traveled at night and rested during the day by finding a "dry place" in the swamp and resting against a tree in a sitting position. Often they would hear the enemy moving close around them on a nearby trail during the day as they rested.

Bloodsucking leeches tore at their flesh and insects feasted on their now bleeding bodies. Their clothing was ragged and torn by the dense jungle growth in the swamps. But they had a strong will to live and kept moving east.

Dwight and Dallas had both undergone intensive survival training and knew how to exist in the swamps. They knew basically which plants were poisonous and which insects and reptiles not to eat. They survived mainly on lizard tails, as the lizards were easily caught. For green vegetables they ate their fill of tree leaves and grass, topped off with grub worms or termites for dessert.

They had no fires, so everything had to be eaten raw. Occasionally, they were able to catch a snake and eat its raw and bloody flesh, thankful to have something to give them strength to keep going. They drank swamp water when there was nothing else. But often, after a rain, they drank fresh rainwater from animal tracks.

Dysentery and the leeches were their worst problems. They lost a lot of blood and suffered terribly from dehydration. After 26 days out in the swamps, they were so weak that traveling was becoming nearly impossible. Dallas was in a bad way as his hand was infected. Dwight was preparing him psychologically for possible amputation of his arm to stay ahead of the infection.

On their 27th day in the swamps Dwight stood up from his resting position against a tree as he thought he heard a noise. He looked carefully around, rifle in hand. Nothing in sight, he relaxed for a moment.

"Frankie, Frankie," a woman's voice called.

Startled, Dwight stood frozen in his tracks. No one except his grandma had ever called him by that name. And no one in the Navy even knew that he had a grand-mother, much less a nickname. He must be hearing things, perhaps the wind in the thick swamp growth.

"Frankie, Frankie," again the voice called.

Dwight immediately recognized the familiar voice of his grandmother.

"That you, Grandma?" Dwight answered back out of long habit, as he turned to the direction of the sound.

Dwight stood staring in disbelief at his grandmother not over seven or eight feet from him. Her long hair was down her back as he had often seen it in the afternoons around the house, and she wore a familiar dress.

"Have you gone and gotten yourself lost, Sonny Boy?" Grandma asked, a pleasant smile about her face.

"Yes, I have, Grandma. I'm in a bad way. I need help," Dwight responded.

"Now, don't worry, Frankie. Just keep your face into the wind. You'll be okay."

Dwight heard a noise just then and turned quickly to see Dallas stirring

from against the tree where he had been sleeping. The sound of voices had awakened him. Dwight turned quickly back to his grandmother, but Grandma was nowhere in sight. Dwight searched but could not find her. There was a stiff breeze blowing from the north as Dwight helped Dallas to his feet. North was the direction of the enemy, but they hurriedly moved north in broad daylight in obedience to Grandma's instructions.

Dwight and Dallas had not gone over 1/2 mile when they came upon the most beautiful sight that two lost forward observers could ever hope to find. Directly in front of them was a whole platoon of U.S. marines.

Dallas was given pain pills and his hand cleaned and bandaged as they waited for choppers already en route to move the marines to headquarters. As the choppers approached, they came under heavy enemy fire. Two pilots were killed while the choppers were on the ground.

When the chopper Dallas and Dwight were in finally lifted off the ground, Dwight noticed that the chopper seemed to hover in the air while being shot to pieces with enemy gunfire.

Dwight screamed out, "Who's flying this thing anyway — a drunk? Somebody get a pilot!"

"The pilot is dead, man. This eggbeater is being flown by a ground pounder who is trying to read the instrument panel," a marine shouted back above the noise of the chopper.

After what seemed hours, the chopper moved out, swaying from side to side, just barely over the tops of the trees, and finally made it to headquarters. There Dwight found a message informing him that his grandmother had died. He looked at the message and compared the date of her death with his notes. Grandma had died exactly seven days before she appeared to him in the swamp. No one will ever convince Dwight F. Fields that he did not hear an angel call his name on that day, so long ago now, in 1967 in the swamps of South Vietnam.

Chapter 5

Angels and Financial Help

When Jacob Kurien finally made it to the airline ticket counter, after waiting in a long line, he reached out of long habit, without thinking, for his billfold, to be ready to pay for his ticket to Nairobi, South Africa. Soon, the clerk gave him the exact price of the round trip ticket. In his billfold he had about $5,000, all in 100 dollar traveler's checks to be used for expenses while in Africa.

Jacob was en route to a meeting which had been planned for well over a year, with much money already spent on advertising. Jacob Kurien, a missionary evangelist, was to be the key speaker for the National Pastor's Conference to be attended by hundreds of pastors, their wives, and members of their congregations. Jacob was to arrive the day before the main meeting for a special meeting, with just the pastors and their wives in attendance. He knew that the money paid to the pastors to attend this meeting had been provided by the small, rural churches at great sacrifice. Few wealthy people attend these churches. Jacob had been looking forward to this very special pastor's conference with great expectations for quite a long while.

Now Jacob eased his hand deep into his right rear pants pocket, but found nothing. The pocket was empty. He quickly checked his other pants pockets only to find that they, too, were empty. In his coat pocket he found his passport and visa, but no billfold, no cash, and no traveler's checks.

Immediate panic gripped Jacob, hit him right in the center of his stomach. It broke him into a cold, clammy sweat. He only had a matter of minutes before the plane's departure, and he had to be on that plane.

Gradually gaining a little more control of himself, he asked for directions to lost and found. Once there, he reported the billfold and money missing. He also solicited the help of airport security personnel in an attempt to locate the billfold as quickly as possible. An officer accompanied Jacob as he retraced his steps by going back to the last place he remembered having the billfold in his possession.

Jacob quickly returned to the restaurant where he had ordered a sandwich and coffee before getting in line to purchase the ticket. No, the restaurant personnel had not seen the billfold. Nor had anyone in the restaurant for that matter. The situation looked hopeless.

Jacob thanked the officer for his help. He then went to a phone booth where he might have some privacy for prayer. What Jacob most needed at this very moment was an outstanding miracle.

Jacob completed his prayer and returned to the ticket counter in the event that the police might locate his billfold before the plane's departure, now only short minutes away. As Jacob approached the ticket counter, he would step aside, let others ahead, then step back to the end of the line to repeat the process all over again.

Soon, Jacob was the last one in line with no others to step aside for. The last tickets for his flight were being sold. As Jacob approached the ticket counter, someone called his name. He turned quickly to his left to retrieve what he hoped would be his billfold containing the money and traveler's checks. A very neatly dressed man in a dark-colored business suit, a handsome man about 30 years old, held a plain white envelope in one hand and an airline ticket in the other.

"Are you Jacob Kurien?" the man asked, while extending the ticket toward Jacob.

"Yes, I am," nodded Jacob somewhat surprised. He had expected the return of his billfold. He had not authorized anyone to take money from his wallet to purchase tickets. Furthermore, there appeared to be no billfold in the stranger's hand.

Jacob managed a weak and state-of-shock type "thank you" as he took the tickets from the handsomely dressed stranger's extended hand. The man then pushed the plain white envelope toward Jacob which he grabbed hurriedly as the last call for boarding the flight for South Africa was blaring out over the sound system.

Jacob quickly turned to check his luggage and obtain a boarding pass, thinking that he would introduce himself and thank the stranger while the luggage was weighed and checked. However, when he turned around, only a few seconds later, the stranger was nowhere to be seen. Jacob was alone. No others were standing around the ticket counter as the last boarding call had been given. Jacob grabbed up his luggage and ran down the main aisle of the building, but was unable to spot the young man. He stopped to question a group of people nearby but no one had seen a man fitting the description. Jacob could not search any longer, he had to board his plane. Safely aboard the plane, he remembered the plain white envelope the stranger had given him. Surely the envelope would contain a letter of explanation, or at the very least, a business card. But in the envelope Jacob found 100, he counted them the second time, 100 crisp, new hundred dollar bills: twice the amount he had lost in traveler's checks. The $5,000 in cash which he had lost in the billfold was replaced with a round trip ticket to Africa.

Jacob had never seen the young man before and has not seen nor heard from him since that incident in the airport. Was the handsomely dressed young man an angel on a mission of mercy, or just someone who wanted to help a stranger in need?

Later after returning from a very successful trip to Africa, Jacob questioned the airport police and discovered that they knew nothing about the incident and had never found his billfold. Was the handsome stranger an angel then? You will never convince Jacob Kurien that he was not an angel sent in answer to his prayer for help. He is thoroughly convinced that angels can and do provide financial assistance.

Chapter 6

The Man Who Talked with Angels

The following story illustrates the incredible work of angels in the life of Roland Buck, an Assemblies of God pastor who co-wrote the 1979 best-seller *Angels on Assignment.* This account is shared by his daughter, Sharon Buck White.

One Monday morning my father walked into my office. This was not unusual, because although he was very busy he would often take a few minutes out of his busy schedule and he and his dog Queenie would stroll down the hall to my office for a little chat.

That particular morning he threw me a bombshell. We were quietly discussing the services the day before, when in the same ordinary tone of voice, Daddy asked me a very extraordinary question. He said, "Honey, what would you say if I told you that I had a visit from an angel last Saturday night?"

I said, "What?"

He repeated, "I had a visit from an angel last Saturday night!"

"Wow!" was my response!

He asked, "Do you believe me?"

I told him, "Of course I do!"

He then began to describe this incredible encounter. I literally hung on every word. I asked him when he was going to share this visit with the congregation. He said he didn't know, and wondered if people would believe him. I told him, "Of course they will!"

Tears began to stream down his cheeks as he continued sharing with me the message the angel had brought from God. Tears filled my eyes, too, as I listened to what my father was saying. He was a man who would never try to be flamboyant or lean toward the sensational just to reach people. He had steered a steady, middle-of-the-road course for many years, not following the different fads that would come and go.

The supernatural work of God through my dad's life didn't begin with the angelic visitations. All through his ministry God would, at different times, let him know areas of need in people's lives as he would shake their hands following a church service. Or God would reveal someone to him as they were involved in something they wouldn't want anyone to know about. Daddy would either immediately go to that person, or tell them later, as God would direct. There were a lot of people who learned how much God cared about what they did or did not do, as He would reveal these things to Dad. God could trust Dad with any information, because unless God released it in his spirit, *no one* else ever knew the secrets God had shown him other than the person involved. He always said that he felt the word of knowledge can be a dangerous thing in the hands of a careless person.

Altogether, he was privileged to experience 27 angelic visitations between June 18, 1978, and October 13, 1979. Eighteen of these are described in the book *Angels on Assignment*.

Early one morning the Holy Spirit told my dad to write the following:

Write, preserve the words which I have spoken to you. They shall become a light to many. I will not only minister through you, but will accompany these words, and give them life wherever sent, even as I have already given wings to My messages brought to you by the angel of the Lord. Fear not to speak in His name, for the words I give are not your words, but His words, and are established forever. Are they not found in His eternal living Word? Long-closed doors of many peoples and nations will be penetrated by these words of life. I command the hosts of the Lord who have been sent forth for this hour to hasten the gathering together unto Him a people for His Name, and to prepare them for that great day of the Lord. They will both precede and follow these words from the Father to make ready the people, to scatter forces of darkness, and to gently care for the multitudes who will hear.

Daddy had this promise from the Lord, so he never tried in any way to help God get the message out that He told him to share with the world. He simply preached the messages to his congregation and left the rest up to God.

Tapes of the messages he preached to his congregation began to circulate around the United States, and were soon being duplicated and sent to Canada and to many countries around the world. Requests came from people who were hungry to hear the messages straight from God's heart, as brought to my father by divine messenger.

The tapes finally reached Charles and Frances Hunter through some friends, and their hearts were thrilled and their spirits quickened by the tremendous messages they heard. God's plan for getting His message out was unfolding through the obedience of the Hunters in responding to the urgency of this message.

Charles and Frances contacted Daddy and their spirits witnessed his genuineness as they spent time sharing with him. These dedicated servants of God worked day and night for the next few months to edit the messages from the tapes. The manuscript flew back and forth between Houston and Boise, and finally on July 5, 1980, the book was ready for distribution in bookstores throughout the United States.

Daddy began to get calls from many places to speak. Following the leading of the Lord, he traveled extensively in the months that followed, sharing in large auditorium meetings, TV programs, and in small fellowships.

People everywhere were finding Jesus. Hundreds of thousands found new hope through the beautiful Bible truths illuminated by divine messenger and shared through the book and tapes.

Over and over, Daddy pointed people to *Jesus*. He told them that every message brought by angelic messenger exalted Jesus by reminding them what the sacrifice of Jesus meant to a lost world. Through this sacrifice, men and women once again could be reconciled with the Father.

The Hunters experienced some persecution, but they too had caught the vision of what God is doing in these last days, and they marched forward with a God-given boldness to fulfill their part in bringing this message to the world.

Daddy was told by divine messenger to ignore the thrusts which were being made at him and at the message contained in the book. The angel referred him to Isaiah 45:9, "Let the potsherd strive with the potsherds of the earth."

The question is asked many times, "Why did God send angelic visitors to Pastor Buck?" His answer to that was, "I don't know why. I probably wouldn't have chosen me if I were God! But God did choose me, and I am simply obeying Him!"

The book by Charles and Frances Hunter, as told to them by my father contains the message that God wants the world to know. In a nutshell, though, the following is the message that was given.

There is good news for you and your family in these last days! God has sent out a host of angels to push, prod, and do whatever is necessary to bring people to a point of choice in accepting what He has done for them through the sacrifice of Jesus. The angels aren't listening to any objections from the individual, and if they don't choose Jesus the first time, then the cycle will start all over again. Angelic forces are on the job.

If you don't know the Lord, and someone from your family is praying for you, you are highly favored of God. He has sent His angels to bring you to a point of choice, because God loves you so much!

The main focus of the messages brought by the angels over and over again is the sacrifice of Jesus. He bore the stroke of God's judgment in His own body. Because of this sacrifice, when men and women accept what He has done, they are restored to their original state of innocence in God's eyes. They are made just as though they had never sinned. They are not pardoned in God's eyes, because pardon means the records are still there, but they are justified, which means made as though they have never sinned.

What does this mean to you? It means when you find Jesus, you are not an ex-alcoholic or an ex-homosexual or an ex-prostitute, but the blood of Jesus covers you, letting God see only the righteousness of Jesus when He looks at you. You are therefore restored to your original state of innocence, as clean and pure in the eyes of the Father as the day you were born. That's what atonement means to you.

Doesn't this make you want to accept the wonderful new life that God offers you through the sacrifice of His Son Jesus? Why not do it right now? Jesus said, "If you call upon My name, you will be saved!" Just say, "Jesus, I accept what You have done for me, I believe in You, and I want to be Your child from now on. Thank You for loving me so much!"

You are now born into the kingdom with a new heart, a new home, and a new life.

Another very important part of what God wants the world to know is that believers will not be at the White Throne Judgment. That judgment is only for those who reject Christ.

When God gathers all His believers around the throne, it will be to say "thanks" for all those things they did to help lift the load for someone. The encouraging word you gave, the plate of cookies you baked, "just because." Things that perhaps in the eyes of the world weren't anything really special, but through God's eyes represented His love being beamed through you to a world that is so hungry and cold and longing for that gentle touch. God will not turn His spotlight on your life at that time looking for the things you did wrong, because all of your sins and failures are covered through the atonement of Jesus.

The angel summed it up this way. "The believers' judgment is not a dark night through which he must pass before he breaks into God's eternal day, but a day in which God has chosen to thank His people!"

Charles and Frances E. Hunter, *Angels on Assignment* (Kingwood, TX: Hunter Books, 1979).

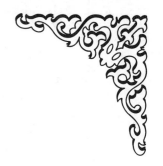

Chapter 7

Moments with Angels

Everybody knows about angels . . . well, at least on some level. And today it seems that more people are talking about angels than ever before. Today there are boutiques devoted to angels, and greeting cards, poetry, songs, and books portraying them in all their goodness. We even take these wonderful "angelic" qualities and apply them to a sweetheart, spouse, kids, or special people.

Billy Graham, in his popular book on angels, states, "Angels have a much more important place in the Bible than the devil and his demons."[1]

The Bible is chock-full of dramatic angelic appearances . . . Abraham, Jacob, Moses, Joshua, Gideon, David, Elijah, Zechariah, Joseph, Mary, and Peter, along with others, saw angels. Angels in the Bible are seen in many roles . . . climbing ladders, wrestling with people, taming lions, lifting great weights, announcing births, recruiting leaders, warriors in battle, executioners, performing miraculous rescues, and comforting people.

Two angels are mentioned by name . . . Michael and Gabriel. Michael is depicted in three biblical books as the "Great Prince" or archangel; Gabriel is shown presiding over paradise.

So, what are angels? We know, according to the Bible, that they are created beings, dignified, majestic, and intelligent. They are personal beings who always represent God, but are not omnipresent, which God is. Little is said of their appearance, but they can take on the physical form of a person and sometimes are mistaken for another human being. The word "angel" simply means "messenger."

They are seen as protectors, messengers ordered by God to minister in a myriad of ways in the Bible.

Some things to note: At no time should an angel or angels be worshiped! The Bible is very clear that only God is to be worshiped. Second, we are not to pray to angels! You might ask God for help in an emergency, but we are never to pray to angels. Let's open our eyes and ears of understanding and ask God to help us develop a healthy balance in regard to His angels.

My mother told me this story about another ministry couple who were contemporaries of theirs, the now deceased Pastor and Mrs. Bennie C. Heinz. At the time of this happening, the Heinz family was pastoring a North Dakota church.

Pastor and Mrs. Heinz and another couple made their way to a springtime fellowship meeting quite a distance away in the town of Dickinson. If I recall correctly, he was one of the speakers. This was one of those all-day affairs . . . morning service, lunch, afternoon service, minister's business meeting, dinner, and finally the evening rally/service. When they left it was approximately 10:30 p.m. as they drove away from the church.

Weather in North Dakota can be very unpredictable in the springtime. They turned north on Highway 85 towards Williston and it started to rain/sleet/snow all at the same time.

They started down into the last valley and the icy mixture continued to fall, but with more intensity. It started to accumulate on the highway, making driving very treacherous. They had no snow tires or chains on the car. Mrs. Heinz began to pray, "Help us, Lord, help our car, keep us safe."

As they began the climb from the valley floor the car began to lose traction and soon they came to a complete stop. No matter what was tried, the car would spin out of control — no traction. Nothing to do but prepare to spend the night huddled in the car.

About that time a car drove up behind them with six husky young men in it. They stopped behind the stalled car and one of them asked if they could be of help.

Pastor Heinz said, "A push would help us, but we really need more traction on the rear end. Perhaps more weight would help."

The pastor started the car and five of these young men began to push the car up the steep road . . . after it got rolling they all jumped up on the trunk. Two were hanging over the sides, the other three were sitting with their feet on the rear bumper. They easily made it.

At the top of the hill Pastor Heinz stopped the car to get out to thank these kind heavyweight strangers. When he stepped out of the car to go to the rear to speak with the men . . . they were all gone! Disappeared! Not a trace! Not a track! Not even of the car in which they had come!

Another happening occurred in a southern state. Eugene and Judy had eight kids ranging in age from 5 to 15. They were a church-going, loving family. Gene had worked at a local lumber mill for years, and when it folded he was left with doing odd jobs for a living.

One day he had a small job in town working on a car. Judy, on this day, was doing the laundry when some church ladies dropped over for a visit.

Their conversation was broken when Judy's oldest came into the house. "Mom, there's a black man coming around to the back door. Says he's got to talk to you."

Immediately these church ladies warned, "Be careful. Don't have anything to do with a man who's comin' begging! Now hear!"

At the back door stood the elderly black man with greying hair and soft, warm eyes. "Ma'am, sorry to bother you, but my truck broke down and I'm walking to town. I would appreciate it if you could give me some water and just a bit of food if you could spare it."

Judy was stunned . . . she found herself hesitant to do the right thing. She had been influenced by the ladies. Instead of getting the water and food she stood there. Eyes met and the old man waited a few seconds and then silently he turned away. Judy felt ashamed as she went back to the table, but worse was the condemning look from her oldest son.

Quickly she grabbed a pitcher of lemonade, some cookies, and ran out the front door to find the old man on his knees with the children around him listening as he was telling them a Bible story. She offered the cookies and lemonade and told him to wait as she went back to prepare a sack lunch. She returned, "I'm sorry about the way I acted."

"That's all right . . . too many people are influenced by others. But unlike some, you have overcome it and this speaks well for you."

That night Gene had wonderful news! The car he had repaired belonged to a man whose brother ran a repair garage and was looking for a mechanic. He hired Gene on the spot!

Later, Judy told Gene about the events of the afternoon. When finished, he asked, "Did you say this was an elderly black man? Kind-looking eyes and gray hair?" He jumped out of bed and went through his pockets until he found a piece of folded paper which he handed to Judy and said, "I met that man walking down the road when I came from town. He waved me over and gave this to me. When I finished reading it, I looked up and he was gone — just disappeared!"

Judy began to cry as she read the note, "Do not forget to entertain strangers, for by so doing some people have entertained angels without knowing it" (Heb. 13:2).[2]

[1] Billy Graham, *Angels: God's Secret Agents* (Irving, TX: Word, Inc., 1991).
[2] Robert Strand, *Moments with Angels* (Green Forest, AR: New Leaf Press, Inc., 1996).

Chapter 8

Angels by Name

Fast-moving clouds threatened April showers as Harley Stafford, F.R. Flora, and I hastened final preparations for the monthly Saturday night meeting of our fledgling NASA chapter of the Full Gospel Business Men's Fellowship International. We stopped off at the Sweden House Restaurant across from NASA's Manned Spacecraft Center in Houston for a quick cup of coffee and for a last minute inspection of the public address system and arrangement of seating. Everything was a-okay. Later, the three of us would go to a back room for an hour of prayer before the evening service.

The year was 1967. I was employed by NASA as staff engineer.

Only a few months before, after sharing my testimony along with astronaut Tom Stafford during an FGBMFI service, I had been asked by Harley Stafford to serve as secretary and treasurer of the newly formed NASA chapter. Harley was president and F.R. Flora was vice-president. Fred Peyton and Gene Gloor later became directors.

I agreed to accept the office with great expectation, but not without much consideration, for I was deeply involved with Rev. Don Anshon in founding a much-needed Teen Challenge Center in Houston. This was taking not only all of my extra hours, but also much of my time reserved for sleep, as we were on the streets on weekends until the early morning hours.

But if our expectation for the NASA chapter was great, God's was even greater. Family relationships were healed. Separated couples were reunited. Teenagers were delivered from drugs. Cripples walked. Many were healed of medically incurable diseases. And after every service, a great number responded to the invitation for salvation. We were experiencing revival.

With faith and expectation running in high victory, F.R. Flora, Harley Stafford, and I finished our third cup of coffee and went to a back room for prayer. Loud claps of thunder reminded us the April showers were well on their way.

"Father, in the name of your blessed Son, Jesus, I rebuke rain and command it to go," Harley prayed. After awhile we heard no more thunder. And when we finished praying we walked outside to enjoy a beautiful sunset, complete with a rainbow before the evening service.

I sat spellbound, along with about 150 others, in the evening service as our speaker shared his testimony. Tom Woodward was a Christian businessman and a member of an Assembly of God church in Pasadena. He shared with us how he had come to know the reality and power of the Holy Spirit.

Not long before, he was showing a Jewish rabbi through his home church one evening. The rabbi had been baptized in the Holy spirit and was to share his testimony with a local FGBMFI chapter that evening.

As they toured Tom's church in Pasadena, it was the time of the men's morning prayer meeting. When they came to the prayer room, they passed quietly so as not to disturb the men who were praying. As they approached the door to leave the room, one of the men began praying very loudly in his heavenly language. Tom moved on as he was accustomed to this type of prayer. However, the rabbi lingered at the door.

After a few moments, Tom approached the rabbi to remind him that it was time to continue as they were to speak before a lady's luncheon and must first return to the motel to dress. But the rabbi placed his finger across his lips for silence. For some 10 to 15 minutes Tom waited. Surely the rabbi had experienced such a thing before. Tom was growing impatient.

But then as he approached the rabbi again, he noticed that the rabbi's countenance had changed. He looked like someone who had seen a ghost. His complexion was white and he had a look of bewilderment.

"What's wrong?" Tom asked.

"Shhh! Silence!" the rabbi commanded.

For a full 30 minutes the rabbi stood in the doorway listening intently to the prayer of the man in the prayer room. After awhile there was silence.

"Who was that man praying to? What languages does he know?" The rabbi queried with demand.

"Why," Tom said, "he is an uneducated man here in the church. He knows no languages other than English. I know him well. I will introduce you so that you may see for yourself."

The rabbi then explained that he had just listened to the most beautiful and perfect Hebrew that he had ever heard spoken. And the rabbi was an astute student of Hebrew. He said for some 15 or 20 minutes the man spoke praises to God in the most beautiful psalms in blank verse.

"But the most amazing thing then happened," the rabbi continued. "Still speaking in perfect Hebrew, the man switched from the psalms and began calling angels by name and sending them on missions. Angels were called by their Hebrew name and were sent to aid missionaries in trouble, the name and location of the missionary being also mentioned in the Hebrew language."

The rabbi was visibly shaken. Never had he even remotely dreamed that such a thing could be possible. And, of course, Tom Woodward required some time to regain his composure.

After our speaker had finished his amazing testimony, I rushed to him, along with all the other 150-some people, for further information. I did manage to talk with him at length later that night. Yes, he was quite positive that the information was accurate just as he had related it. And, yes, if I so desired it would be possible for me to talk with the rabbi.

Thus, I began my long research and intensive investigation into the ministry of God's angels. So intrigued was I that I can remember that Saturday years ago as clearly as if it had been only a few days. It seems the Holy spirit so entrenched the message in my spirit that I can remember every word that was spoken.

But my dilemma was in not being able to accept what was said because I could find no scriptural basis for such a relationship between God's angels and the believers. If it were not in the Bible, then I could not accept it, no matter who said it. But, yet, I knew it had to be true. It was simply the reporting of a supernatural fact by God's kids. The fact was reported with no explanation and this left me hanging. I must have scriptural proof. But no scriptural proof was offered that night.

I walked around in a daze for at least two weeks. I felt that I was right on the frontier of understanding some of the great mysteries which Paul perhaps had in mind when he wrote Ephesians 1:15-17.

What intrigue! What mystery! If believers actually had at their disposal the armies of heaven, God's angels, then this surely explained the invincibility of the Church which Jesus referred to in Matthew 16:18.

Of course, I knew that angels were supernatural beings available to help the believer at times. At least they had done so in biblical days. I knew this in a vague sort of way. The very thought of a believer calling God for the aid of an angel sent goose bumps racing up and down my spine! And it still does. But now I know that it can be and is being done. And now I know the scriptural basis for it.

But I learned these things only after talking with hundreds of people about their experiences with angels. And after I had spent a great many hours in prayer and much time in the Scriptures. God's Word gave me the answers. The Holy Spirit explained them to me.

Chapter 9

Angel at the Door

For months following the amazing testimony of the angels, I searched for a biblical explanation. I talked with ministers. I searched for books on angels, but found none. Nor did I find anyone who could satisfactorily explain the relationship between the believer and God's angels.

"Yes, I believe God could send angels to help if it were necessary," a minister said, "but we don't see angels today because we have the Holy Spirit now and angels aren't needed as they were during biblical times."

But yet there were many references to angels in the Book of Acts, and the Early Church certainly had the Holy Spirit. And the need in our time was no less than it had been in biblical times. Furthermore, I had no proof that angels were not often being seen in our day.

And as for the question of any authority that the believer might have to enlist the aid of angels, such a suggestion was unthinkable according to many ministers. I was advised to forget the whole thing.

But forget I could not. The Holy Spirit would not allow it. I was gently awakened from a sound sleep on many nights, and would slip down beside my bed and quietly pray. During these times of great inspiration, the Holy Spirit began speaking to me and encouraging me in my search for truth and understanding.

I knew that someone was going to rise in our time and understand the mystery of God's heavenly armies. I knew God was preparing a people to enter into it. I had a conviction that this was the eleventh hour message, the message for the Church today.

While I was praying by my bed one night, the Holy Spirit whispered in my ear:

In the troubled days that lie ahead, it is going to require all that God can give to you, and be to you, to stand the tests you will go through. God's army of angels is available to every believer.

Satan, knowing his days are shortened, is coming to the earth with all his host, and man is going to pass into a period of spiritual conflict such as the church has never known. This will not only be in persecution, but it will be demons attempting to break and crush the spirit of the Church and the individual believer. The Church must learn the secret of standing against the hosts of darkness in the name of Jesus and by calling on God for the use of angelic armies.

Unable to find current information on angels, I began searching into my own past and reviewing what I had learned. As long as I could remember, I had heard stories about angels. Dad used to tell me bedtime Bible stories, and many of these included angels. One of my favorite stories was Dad's own experience with an angel.

As a young man in high school and later in college, Dad was quite an athlete. As star quarterback on both high school and college football teams, he would run out on the field before the game, jump in the air turning a complete somersault and land on his feet still running.

During a particularly rough game in college, Dad was hit with a flying tackle and a vertebrae in his neck was fractured. While in the hospital recovering from these injuries, he was visited by members of the Sabine Tabernacle in Beaumont. They prayed for his healing and began witnessing to him concerning his salvation.

Dad gave his heart to Jesus, and was healed while in the hospital. He then began attending Sabine Tabernacle, a church founded by R.T. "Dad" Richey during his great healing crusades and later pastored by Rev. Harry H. Hodge.

Soon Dad felt a call to the ministry. However, his parents were greatly disappointed as they had other plans for him.

Because of the pressure received at home, Dad ignored the call he felt for the ministry. He took a job with the Magnolia Refinery in Beaumont, Texas, but continued attending Sabine Tabernacle.

He ministered often on Sundays in various churches in the surrounding area and was urged by church members, as well as the Holy Spirit, to begin a full-time ministry. He became miserable on his job, but was reluctant to leave because of his family's strong desires for him to return to college and prepare for a career.

Dad fell from a scaffold while at work and was seriously injured. Part of the injury was a recurrence of problems incurred while playing football. He felt the accident resulted from his disobedience in not heeding God's call to the ministry.

Friends and family urged him to take the matter to court. One uncle even brought a lawyer to the hospital to talk to Dad. Dad went so far as to sign power of attorney over to the lawyers to begin legal action.

However, after returning home and recovering from the accident, Dad had second thoughts about the lawsuit. He felt the accident resulted as mainly a re-injury of an old wound from football days and was not entirely due to the recent accident. But more important to him, he was sure the accident was permitted by God to get him out of the refinery and into the ministry.

Dad was up until early hours of the morning meditating on these things and trying to make a decision about going ahead with the lawsuit against the refinery. There was a large screened porch across the back of the old three-story French home in Beaumont and Dad sat on this porch in a swing.

However, there was no peace in his spirit in going ahead with litigation. He knew that God had placed a call on his life and that he must obey that call. He wanted to be sure he was making a decision in keeping with God's will.

After awhile Dad looked up from prayer and noticed a brilliant glowing white light in the garden which appeared to be moving. The light took form directly in front of the screen door. An angelic appearance, around eight feet in height with white hair and glowing white garments, stood looking at him.

Dad sat frozen with fear. The angel raised his right hand, pointed straight at Dad, and said in a very commanding voice, "You're a chosen vessel. You have been commanded of God."

With those words the angel disappeared. For several minutes Dad was afraid to move. He knew he had seen an angel. There could be no other explanation. He consequently dropped the lawsuit and later entered the ministry. He was miraculously healed of all injuries.

The appearance of the angel became one of the motivating forces behind Dad's ministry. He could never doubt that God had called, no matter how difficult the trials of life in the ministry became.

Chapter 10

Dining with an Angel

My wife, Jane, also was familiar with angels because of an experience her mother had with an angel while a young girl still living at home. Together, we began reviewing our past experiences and familiarity with angels along with the scriptural references.

Jane's mother had often told the story of the day the angel visited Cameron, Texas. But since Jane is more familiar with the account she will tell it in her own words, just as her mother used to relate it to Jane when she was a child.

It was the year 1935.

Fiery, and saturated with the love and power of the Great Almighty, aggressive and zealous to preach the Word without fear or favor, Rev. Harry H. Hodge took the gospel to the small town of Cameron, Texas.

"Ye must be born again!" He shouted out the words like a sonic boom loudly and clearly while standing atop milk cases stacked three high in the small town park.

Like the devils in the Bible, Jesus I know and Paul I know, but who in the world is this fellow making such a show? A total stranger he was, but it didn't take long for the crowd to gather 'round and listen intently to what this Bible-waving, boisterous-voiced saint had to proclaim.

He was, for a fact and without a moment's doubt, a preacher if ever there lived one. And never, in all the history of Cameron, had the folks of that small, quiet, peaceful town ever witnessed such a fervor, sincerity, diligence, and vehemence in the delivery of a gospel sermon.

The impact upon the people that day could be likened unto the Day of

Pentecost (save a few thousand). Right there in the town park as Brother Hodge delivered his soul, men and women fell on their faces before God and repented of their sins lest they die and go straight to hell "where forever there would be weeping and wailing and gnashing of teeth and the worm dieth not."

Indeed, revival broke out and spread for miles around. Skeptics, spectators, sinners, and saints gathered nightly for the hand-clapping, foot-stomping, Jericho-marching, Bible-preaching, hallelujah services.

Soon a church was erected known as the Sabine Tabernacle. The revival continued to spread with enthusiasm and the church continued to grow. As the old-timers of early Pentecost have been noted for saying, "It's better felt than telt."

Traveling evangelists began to make their way to the town of Cameron and it was told that there was a certain family who would, with great delight, feed the travelers and lodge them. This was a rather large family of five boys, and just enough girls, two — one to do the cooking and one to do the dishes.

It wasn't an unusual thing at all for this Hayes family to entertain strangers almost daily, but one day a different sort of stranger came calling.

Lucille Hayes, the younger of the two girls, welcomed the caller, and, as was their friendly custom, immediately offered him something to eat.

As the traveler dined, he and Lucille made conversation, but of nothing in particular. Upon finishing his meal, he offered thanks, picked up his hat, and said he must be on his way. Lucille walked him to the door and bid him farewell. Just before walking out, the stranger turned and looked straight at Lucille; his eyes had a great depth and an unusual brightness and seemed to look right through her.

"God bless you and this household," the stranger said finally, and then he turned quickly and was gone.

Closing the screen door, Lucille moved to the window nearby so she could prop herself and watch which way the man was traveling. He was nowhere to be seen. He hadn't even had time to reach the steps of the porch, much less move rapidly enough to be gone from sight.

Lucille looked in unbelief and immediately made her way outside. He was not there! She ran out into the yard and looked down the road, first to the left and then to the right. He just wasn't there. He wasn't anywhere!

Lucille excitedly related the experience to Rev. Harry Hodge, who assured her that she had been visited by one of God's holy angels appearing in human form as they often did in the Bible days.

"It was an angel sent from God to bring a blessing to you and your family for the great work you are doing for the church here in Cameron," Hodge assured her, taking his Bible and pointing to a Scripture, "Be not forgetful to entertain strangers: for thereby some have entertained angels unawares" (Heb. 13:2).

Chapter 11

Angel by a Bus Stop

I had several very unusual experiences with the power of God the year I turned 13. Although I grew up in church, I had never experienced salvation.

One night very late when other family members were in bed, I knelt in my room and began praying. I was asking God to help me catch a calf in the calf scramble which was a few weeks away. I had been reading my Bible and underlining certain Scriptures in the New Testament pertaining to God's miracle power.

My name had been selected through the 4-H Club from hundreds of entries. There were to be twice as many boys as calves turned loose in a rodeo arena. I had only a 50 percent chance at best, but actually less, because boys up to 21 years of age could enter. Thirteen was the youngest age eligible.

As I knelt in prayer, I began asking God to show me if He were real, to give me some sign. I asked for Jesus to forgive me of my sins and to come into my heart.

Soon the whole room became illuminated with a supernatural light. I experienced a great peace and joy. It flooded my whole being. I felt an assurance that God was with me, indeed, and that He would help me in catching a calf.

I prayed not only for a calf, but I asked God somehow to lead me to the calf that would become champion.

The Saturday morning of the calf scramble I caught a city bus to my grandmother's home. I was to work in her yard that morning and then ride with my Dad to the rodeo arena and state fairgrounds for the calf scramble that afternoon.

My grandmother lived on the other side of Beaumont, Texas, and this required that I transfer buses downtown. While on Pearl Street at the bus stop, waiting, along with several other people for a south-bound bus, I was approached by a black man. He had apparently been at the edge of the sidewalk up against a building, as I had not seen him at first.

He touched me on the arm and asked for a quarter. A quarter was all I had so I tried to ignore him by not looking at him. But he was persistent.

I turned to look at him. He was neatly dressed, not looking at all like a beggar. There was a shine, almost like a radiance, about his face. I had noticed this same sort of radiance on the faces of people at church who had been praying for some time.

When I turned him down, his face saddened. "It is very important for you to give me a quarter," he said. He did not say why he needed a quarter, nor did I ask. An ordinary beggar would have had some sort of sob story. But this fellow offered none.

Reluctantly, I reached into my pocket and pulled out my only quarter — all of my money. As I laid the quarter in his palm, his hand tightened around mine. He held my hand for what seemed like minutes as he looked straight into my eyes. A strange feeling encompassed me. I remember thinking, *This can be no ordinary man.*

And then, still looking straight into my eyes, he said, "God bless you."

With that, he turned and walked down the street. A bus was approaching and I looked to see if it was my bus. I glanced again and ran quickly toward the rear to look up and down the sidewalk as the bus passed by. But nowhere could the stranger be found. And there were no doorways or alleys for him to have entered.

The strange feeling persisted all morning as I worked for my grandmother. That afternoon at the rodeo as the calves were being unloaded for the scramble, a melody kept going through my mind.

> Only believe, only believe;
> All things are possible, only believe.
> Only believe, only believe;
> All things are possible, only believe.
> Lord, I believe. Lord, I believe.
> All things are possible. Lord, I believe.[1]

As the boys were lining up in the arena, the melody kept going through my mind. The calves were run into the arena on the opposite side. The boys crouched with eager anticipation, rope halters tucked neatly in their belts.

BOOM! The starter gun broke the silence with deafening finality. It was now or never for 60 boys trying to catch 30 wild calves fresh off the range.

I heard the gun but saw or heard nothing else. It was as if I had gone into a trance. I completely blanked out. When I came to, I had my arms locked around a huge black Angus calf. The calf was dragging me around the arena. I had no idea how I could have gotten my arms around the calf. I remembered only hearing the starter gun.

I was brought back to reality by a friend screaming for me to put my halter on the calf. The calf was so large I had great difficulty dragging him across the finish line, even with the halter in place.

That evening after I had gotten the calf home and acquainted with his new mother, a cream-colored Jersey milk cow, I had time to think.

The words of the stranger were still burning in my heart and I knew that this experience was somehow related to the miraculous way in which I had caught the calf.

I knelt in the barn beside the nursing calf and thanked God for His blessings. But I told no one about the strange experiences.

A few weeks later my nurse cow became seriously ill will acetonemia, an ailment not uncommon in those days with high-producing milk cows. A veterinarian was called to treat the cow and she seemingly recovered.

However, a few days later as I was allowing the calf to nurse early one morning before school, before my eyes the nurse cow fell in a heap and stiffened. She showed no movement of any kind and not the faintest hint of any breathing.

The calf backed away and then nudged the cow on the side. Still there was no movement. I pulled the calf away.

My heart sank within me and a great fear began to creep over me. I had no money to purchase another milk cow. And without the cow I would not even be allowed to keep the calf, let alone win the championship I had been praying for.

Bitter tears made their way down my cheeks. I cried with the great heaves of a broken heart. The calf nudged my side.

I fell limply on the barn floor asking God why He had allowed this to happen. After awhile I arose from prayer and turned to leave. I would need to feed the calf on powdered milk with a bucket until the calf scramble officials could make arrangements to give him to someone else.

At the barn door I turned and looked back at the cow. Without thinking about it and for no reason, I pointed the index finger of my right hand straight at the cow and said, "In the name of Jesus, I command you to rise and live!"

The strange words came from my lips but it seemed another person down inside of me actually spoke the words. Almost as if time had turned back, the cow scrambled to her feet and resumed eating from the trough in front of her. From the other side of the barn, the calf ran quickly to the cow and continued to nurse. It seemed nothing had actually happened but all was a dream. But I knew the cow had died. The outline of her body was in the sawdust floor where she had fallen.

As I walked home through the pasture that morning, puzzling over the strange events, the parting words of the stranger with the shining black face came back to me. "God bless you," he had said.

Later that year my calf was awarded the banner at the South Texas State Fair for SCRAMBLE CHAMPION STEER CALF. At an early age I learned God's Word cannot fail and angels do minister unto us.

[1] "Only Believe," music and words by Paul Rader, copyright 1921, renewal 1949 by Mary C. Rader. Assigned to Rodeheaver Company. Used by permission.

Chapter 12

Angels in the Old Covenant

Continuing my search of the Scriptures for the relationship of angels to the New Testament believer, I began studying the blood covenant God had made with Abraham, Isaac, and Jacob. I was astonished to discover that Abraham knew that God had actually sent an angel with his servant to prosper the servant in locating a wife suitable for his son Isaac (Gen. 24:7, 40).

Then I read in Daniel 10:12 that the angel told Daniel he had come at the command of God because Daniel had requested his coming. What astounding information! What possible right could these early men have to request the services of God's heavenly creatures? Such a thing was almost unthinkable. But there it is in black and white in God's own Word.

When the nation Israel was in great distress, her elders called on God for deliverance. God answered according to their words and sent an angel at their request. For we read in Numbers 20:16, "And when we cried unto the Lord, he heard our voices and sent an angel, and hath brought us forth out of Egypt: and, behold, we are in Kadesh, a city in the uttermost of thy border."

Then I made another startling discovery in the Old Testament. I found that according to Ezekiel the Holy Spirit has supervision over the angels, at least to some extent. I read in Ezekiel 1:12 and 1:20 that the angels moved as directed by the Holy Spirit. This would seem to explain why a man on earth praying in his heavenly language "as the Spirit gave utterance" could call on angels and send them on special missions.

Then I began to get some insight into the relationship these old covenant men enjoyed with angels. In Exodus I read in the special blood covenant God cut with Abraham that provision was made for the angels to minister for Israel, God's blood covenant people.

In Exodus 23:20, I read, "Behold, I send an Angel before thee, to keep thee in the way, and to bring thee into the place which I have prepared." And Exodus 23:23, "For mine Angel shall go before thee."

In this same chapter of Exodus other covenant blessings were mentioned, such as, "I will take sickness away from the midst of thee. There shall nothing cast their young, nor be barren, in thy land: the number of thy days I will fulfill" (Exod. 23:25-26).

Yes, the promise of the angel was definitely a part of the covenant blessing. There could be no doubt about it. David talked about these covenant angels in Psalm 91 and also in Psalm 103.

Daniel said God had sent His angel and shut the lion's mouths, thus saving Daniel's life. What secret did Daniel know? Why, he knew he was a covenant man covered by the covenant God had made with Abraham, Isaac, and Jacob. Daniel had a right to expect God to send His delivering angels.

But just what was this mysterious covenant of blessing, I wondered. Few sermons had ever been preached on it. At that time, no books had been written on the covenant. There had to be something greatly significant about the Abrahamic covenant because it was often referred to in the Bible, both in the Old and New Testaments.

In studying the covenant, I found that some immensely striking events occurred before God entered into the covenant with Abraham. Among these was the changing of Abram's and Sarai's names to Abraham and Sarah. Prince and princess of God. In other words, God lifted Abraham and Sarah into the royal family before He entered a covenant relationship with them.

When Abraham was 99 years old, God appeared to him as *El Shaddai* or God Almighty.

God said, "Walk before me and be thou perfect. And I will make my covenant between me and thee, and will multiply thee exceedingly."

The 99-year-old Abraham fell flat on his face as God continued. "As for me, behold, my covenant is with thee, and thou shalt be the father of a multitude of nations."

Genesis 15:6 says, "Abraham believed in the Lord; and it was counted to him for righteousness." From the Hebrew, the word *believe* here means an "unqualified committal." God told him to take an animal, God's substitute, and slay it. God then requested that Abraham circumcise himself. Abraham's blood was mingled with the blood of God's substitute.

Think of it! Man's blood was mixed with God's blood to create a new race of people. For the first time in the history of the world there came into being a peculiar race of people called by the name of the Lord.

God and Abraham had entered the blood covenant relationship that was to assure the existence of Israel for eternity. This covenant meant that all Abraham would ever have was laid on the altar. Everything he owned or would ever become belonged irrevocably to God.

But, it also meant that as God's own property, God must put everything under His command at the disposal of Abraham for his use when needed. It meant God must sustain and protect Abraham to the very limit.

God and man had become as one. It was similar to the marriage relationship of husband and wife. When an enemy attacked Abraham's nation Israel, it was as if God himself was being attacked. Therefore, God's heavenly armies of angels were sent to battle for Israel.

An enemy making war with the nation Israel actually went to battle against God. Invincible supernatural soldiers were fought against. This explains why Israel could never be beaten in battle as long as they kept the covenant. There were not enough forces in the allied armies of the world to take even one small village.

When armies of Assyria marched down on the little hamlet of Dothan where Elisha the prophet lived, God's armies were there also. Elisha prayed and God opened the spiritual eyes of His servant so that the young man would not be afraid. The hills surrounding Dothan were covered with warrior angels in chariots. The Assyrian army was surrounded by the armies of heaven.

How did Elisha know the angels were there since they were invisible to the natural eye? He had requested them according to his covenant right! How else would he know they were there?

God sent blindness to the Assyrian army, and one earthly covenant man was able to capture the complete army of a nation. Israel could not be beaten in battle, even when without an earthly army.

Protection and deliverance by angels was available not only to the nation Israel but to individual citizens as well. For we read in Psalm 34:7, "The angel of the Lord encampeth round about them that fear him, and delivereth them."

Every man, woman, and child covered by the covenant was entitled to the ministry of God's angels. This was part of the covenant blessing. *Assistance by God's angels was something to be expected, not the unusual.*

When the Prophet Elijah was running from the wicked queen who sought to kill him, an angel appeared as he slept under a juniper tree.

"Arise, and eat," the angel said. The angel brought a hot plate lunch directly from the kitchen of heaven. Again, the angel brought Elijah a meal of angel's food. On the strength of these meals, Elijah was able to travel for 40 days with no food. God was keeping His covenant to protect and sustain the descendants of Abraham, now citizens of Israel.

But that great legal document, the blood covenant, came into being through the obedience of one man — Abraham.

When Abraham's miracle son, Isaac, was around 20 years of age, God said, "Take now thy son, thine only son Isaac, whom thou lovest, and get thee into the land of Moriah; and offer him there for a burnt offering" (Gen. 22:2).

All heaven looked on in wonder. Angels stood ready for word from God. Would the covenant be ratified by earth man? Or would it now be broken and nullified?

Remember, because Abraham believed God, or made an all-out commitment to God, it was counted to him as righteousness. Believing, trusting Abraham took young Isaac on a journey of three days and three night to the mountain Moriah. Together, they built an altar, bathed, in all probability, by the loving father's tears.

Abraham laid his son on the altar and drew back the sword.

"Abraham! Abraham! stay thy hand!" shouted an angel who had suddenly appeared. A ram from the flocks of heaven was provided for the sacrifice.

All of heaven rejoiced. Angels burst forth in great singing. At long last God had found a man who would keep the covenant. From that moment forward the blood covenant was in full force, completely satisfied by earth man and stamped with God's seal of approval in the Supreme Court of the universe.

From that day forward, there could be no backing down. God had bound Himself to the covenant for eternity. An "everlasting forever." The covenant was an irrevocable agreement between God and man.

The covenant forever. The covenant was the most solemn thing that a man could conceive. For God said, "By myself have I sworn" (Gen. 22:16-17). God's throne became the surety of His promise. God could not break the covenant and man dare not.

Circumcision became the seal of the covenant. All males under the covenant carried the mark of God in their flesh.

We may think of the covenant as similar to the Constitution of the United States. It was a legal document issued by the Supreme Court of heaven and a part of the Constitution of the Universe.

Just as the armies of the United States back our Constitution, the armies of heaven, God's angels, were employed to enforce the blood covenant in behalf of God's new race of people.

We may think of the angels as God's Covenant Enforcing Agents (CEA). God's CEA constantly watch over the covenant to insure that it remains in effect.

According to Galatians 3:19, the angels ordained the law of the covenant. The word ordained here is used in the same sense as administered. In other words, the angels executed or managed the covenant. They watched over the covenant to ensure that its provisions were upheld.

When Israel kept the covenant provision, the CEA worked in their behalf. But when the covenant was broken, the CEA enforced the covenant against Israel to protect God's rights.

The covenant carried both a curse and a blessing. Moses wrote the Law which became man's copy of the legal wording of the covenant. The blessings and curses of the covenant are outlined in Deuteronomy 28 and Leviticus 26.

The blessings of the covenant are surprising, enough to take one's breath away.

God had placed himself under obligation to shield Israel from the armies of the nations that surrounded them. God saw to it that their land brought forth abundant crops. Their herds multiplied exceedingly. No female could cast forth her young before her time. They enjoyed 100 percent calf crops.

Israel became the head of the nations in wealth, and Jerusalem became the richest city the world has ever known. Israel's hillsides were irrigated and her valleys teemed with wealth.

There has been no nation, no city, like it before or since. They were God's own covenant people and Jehovah was their God.

Israel's warriors had great physical strength and prowess. They enjoyed divine protection that made them the greatest soldiers the world has ever known.

One soldier in war could put a thousand to flight. Without weapons they could rend a lion as though it were a kid.

In King David's day when the covenant was a living force in the land, Israel had blood covenant warriors who could individually slay 800 enemy soldiers in a single combat.

Israel became God's peculiar people. They were the treasure of His heart, the apple of His eye.

And the armies of heaven, God's angels, were on standby 24 hours a day to invoke severe punishment upon any earth man, or devil, who attempted to interfere with Israel's covenant blessings.

Chapter 13

Our New Covenant Right to Use Angels

For years I had heard that the Jews enjoyed God's special blessings. It was explained that because of these special blessings the Jews were often wealthy. The Jews were God's chosen people.

But the poor New Testament believer, I was made to understand, was to go through this life persecuted and downtrodden. They could not expect to receive a physical blessing while here on earth. Someday . . .we would all go to heaven and receive our reward.

I began searching the Scriptures for a link between the Abrahamic covenant of the Old Testament and the New Testament believer. Somehow in my spirit I knew God would not provide such great blessings for Israel and leave out the believer.

In recent years I have heard Bible teachers make reference to sending out angels to minister for them. But no one has ever offered any scriptural proof as basis for attempting such a thing. And, although I sensed in my spirit that it was right, I would never pray in that manner regarding angels without a scriptural basis for it.

I have found that every time God reveals something to me through the Holy Spirit, He always provided the scriptural background for the truth revealed. The Scriptures may not always come at the time the revelation or insight is given, but when I ask Him for scriptural proof, it is always forthcoming.

Much can be revealed to us through the realm of our spirit if we learn to teach our minds to receive revelation knowledge without reacting against it. For example, the apostle Paul wrote much of the New Testament and nearly all of the revelations concerning the office and ministry of the risen Christ. How did he know those mysterious things? He had never been with Jesus during His earthly ministry.

Paul received this information from the Holy spirit by revelation. That is, the Holy Spirit living within his own human spirit revealed the information to him. It was Spirit-revealed knowledge, or revelation knowledge, in contrast to sense knowledge, or knowledge gained through the five human senses.

Paul said that when his spirit prayed, he prayed beyond the realm of understanding of his mind. In other words, when the apostle Paul prayed in his heavenly language, his mind did not comprehend what was being said. However, Paul said he could pray and ask God for the interpretation of what he prayed in his heavenly language. And then what he had prayed in his heavenly language would be revealed to him (1 Cor. 14:13-14).

On many occasions I have experienced what Paul was referring to. I have prayed over some problem or difficult situation in my heavenly language and then prayed out the interpretation in English. On several occasions some very shocking information was revealed to me. Something completely opposite of what I was thinking. Often solutions to difficult problems were revealed to me in that manner.

The Spirit has all knowledge; He will lead you into all truth, will teach you all things, the Bible says. The third member of the executive Godhead abides within you if you have received the baptism of the Holy Spirit. Let Him work for you.

As I was praying one day concerning angels and my right to use them, the Holy Spirit spoke very clearly. It was as if someone were in the room speaking to me.

The Holy spirit said, "How many times have you requested the ministry of angels when you were praying in other tongues and you never knew what you had done?"

The thought was startling. I had never conceived of such a thing as being possible. But I remembered Paul said we speak with the tongues of men and angels (1 Cor. 13:1). If we at times spoke with the tongues of angels when praying in our heavenly language, was it not possible for us at such times to request the services of God's heavenly creatures?

Again, as I was praying, the Holy Spirit spoke, "Have you not read where Paul said that you are a registered citizen in Heaven? As a citizen of heaven enjoying full rights and privileges, do you not think you could call on God for angels whose purpose is to minister for those who are the heirs of salvation? As a citizen of the United States and a resident of Houston, would you hesitate to call for the Houston police department or fire department if you were in trouble? If you are in trouble and need supernatural help, why should you not call on God for His heavenly angels?" (Eph. 2:19; Heb. 12:23).

A bright light ignited in my understanding; my spirit understood fully and my mind was beginning to.

In Ezekiel I had read where the Holy Spirit had supervised the activity of angels. Certainly it was reasonable for the Holy Spirit abiding within the believer to exercise some supervision over angels.

I was beginning to understand the believer's right to use angels. But I wanted proof of the believer's relationship and right to use angels beyond reasonable doubt. Considering the Bible a legal document, I asked God to reveal to me Scriptures that would present a sound legal case.

Charles G. Fenney was an attorney, as well as, perhaps, the most successful revivalist and theologian in America. Fenney said that he interpreted all Bible passages as if he were reading a law book. He is said to have stressed the need for fair principles of interpretation as are used in courts of justice.

My uncle, Willard L. Russell, was a noted attorney in Houston, as well as the author of a number of books. Several of his books included extensive research concerning legal grounds for acceptance of the Bible. His first book, *Peace and Power Within* is widely used as a textbook in colleges and universities.

I consulted legal help in my research. It was decided that I should use worldwide adopted rules of interpretation which are a part of the rules of evidence which have accumulated through the centuries for safeguarding the mental process of the judge in determining the true facts in a controversy. These rules of evidence relate primarily to two factors: admissibility of the evidence, and credibility of the witnesses and sufficiency of the proof.

Using the above rules, my uncle and I determined that when an old covenant provision is renewed in new covenant, then, we may safely assume the promise was intended for the benefit of the New Testament believer. My uncle explained it simply by comparing the old and new covenants to a land deed. These are both covenants or legal instruments conveying the rights of parties.

Nearly all of us have at one time or another held a title deed to a house or a piece of land. We may think of the deed which the former owner held as the old covenant and the new deed conveying the property to us as the new covenant.

If the former owner sold us 25 acres out of his 100 acres, then the new deed made out to us would contain a legal description listing 25 and not 100 acres. Also, there would be perhaps certain other restrictions not contained in the original deed. Certain easement rights, for example, might be retained by the former owner and these would be mentioned in the new deed.

In other words, certain benefits or rights would be conveyed by the original owner to the new owner, while others would be retained by the original owner. But in all cases, those things conveyed, or not conveyed, would be clearly detailed in the new deed.

In most states, those things not specifically excluded in the new deed, but contained in the original deed, are considered conveyed by the original owner to the new owner. For instance, if the original owner held all mineral rights on his land and conveys the land by deed to a new owner, but does not specifically reserve mineral rights in the new deed, then all minerals held by the original owner are assumed to go to the new owner.

Now, using these rules of interpretation, let's continue with our study of angels in the covenant. We have seen that under the old covenant, Israel was assured protection by God's angels. Also, individuals, on occasion, actually requested the service of angels. In other words, Israel as a nation had at her disposal the armies of heaven, God's angels. This was part of Israel's covenant blessing. Individual citizens were assured protection and service by angels under the covenant, and there are numerous examples of angels ministering for both Israel and the individual citizen in the Old Testament.

If we can show that those parts of the old covenant promising the ministry of angels are also contained in the new covenant, then we can safely assume that the New Testament believer has the same opportunity for angelic help as Abraham did when God sent an angel to prosper his servant in locating a wife for his son Isaac. In addition, if we can show individuals in the New Testament enjoyed the same authority to use angels as was displayed in the Old Testament, then we can safely conclude that those in the New Testament period full well understood their rights and privileges concerning the ministry of angels. Further, we may safely conclude that we, today, have the same legal right and relationship to angels as that demonstrated by those in the New Testament.

First, we notice that according to Hebrews 7:22 and 8:6, Jesus is the surety of the new covenant and it is called a better covenant than the old covenant. Now if the new covenant is better than the old, it is unreasonable to assume that it provides anything less than that provided Israel in the old covenant. We also notice, then, God was the surety of the old covenant, for He said, "By myself I have sworn," but Jesus is the surety of the new covenant.

In Galatians 3 we read that all of the blessings of the Abrahamic covenant are provided for the believer in the new covenant. Galatians 3:14 reads, "That the blessing of Abraham might come on the Gentiles through Jesus Christ . . ." and Galatians 3:29 says, "If ye be Christ's, then are ye Abraham's seed, and heirs according to the promise."

In fact, the entire New Testament is founded on the Abrahamic and Davidic covenants. From the first chapter of the New Testament to the very last chapter there are many covenant links to both of these covenants.

The Davidic covenant is simply a continuation or expansion of the Abrahamic covenant. There is not sufficient space to discuss the Davidic covenant here, nor is it within the scope of this writing. Both covenants are eternal and closely linked. The essential elements of God's covenant with David are that David's throne would be established forever and that Christ would be born from David's seed (2 Sam. 7:10-17; 1 Chron. 17:11-14).

In contrasting the old and new covenant, we find that an animal was provided as a substitute for God's blood covenant with Abraham. But in the new covenant, God's human son, Jesus Christ, was the sacrifice, and since He was both God and man, the sacrifice contained both God's blood and man's blood. According to Hebrews 9:12, Jesus carried His own blood to offer before the Holy of Holies in the heavens. When the blood of Jesus was accepted by the Father, then the new covenant was ratified and sealed with the blood of the first man of the race of a redeemed people. A people to become known as the sons of God.

The old priestly order was established and Jesus became the new High Priest. He is now the glorified, but still human, Son of God, seated at the Father's right hand "ever living to make intercession for us."

When God accepted the blood of Jesus, He signified that the claims of justice had been met and that man could be legally taken from Satan's authority. Fellowship with the Father could be restored.

Jesus, by His own words, said that He possesses all authority in heaven and earth. He further stated that we could ask anything in His name and He would do it for us. The "all authority" that Jesus now has most assuredly includes authority over angels. Through the name and authority of Jesus, all of heaven's ability, heaven's glory, and heaven's strength are at the disposal of the new covenant believer. This is the most marvelous thing the world has ever seen. All of heaven's resources are available to back the believer because of our new blood covenant relationship with the Father.

Romans 5:17 tells us that we reign as kings in this life by Christ Jesus. We are to absolutely reign as Christ and with Christ right here on earth. How do we do it? By faith in His name. The name above every power whether in heaven, earth, or hell. And we reign with Him. That is part of our covenant blessing.

In Acts 7:53 we find a New Testament reference to angels carrying out administrative duties of the old covenant. Then in Hebrews 1:14 we learn the angels minister for the New Testament believers. "Are they not all ministering spirits, sent forth to minister for them who shall be heirs of salvation?" This parallels Psalm 103:20-21.

Jesus said a very startling thing just before His crucifixion and right after Peter had tried to deliver Him by use of the sword. Jesus announced to the disciples, as if they should already know it, that He could request 12 legions of angels to deliver Him from the hands of Satan. "Thinkest thou that I cannot now pray to my Father, and he shall presently give me more than twelve legions of angels?" (Matt. 26:53).

Now Jesus was human, every bit a man. He knew all of the human limitations. Had He not been human, it would have been futile for God the Father to have sent Him to earth. For He had to redeem fallen man from the act of high treason committed by the first man Adam. Jesus was called the Second Adam. And here we have the human Jesus, by His own words admitting that He had the authority, the covenant right, to request the aid of God's heavenly armies, the angels.

Jesus said the things He did, we would do also. In other words, when Jesus was on earth, He operated completely within His human limitations. He did not have the legal, covenant right to do anything the New Testament believer cannot do. If Jesus could request the aid of angels, so can the new covenant believer.

The Jews have a tradition concerning Adam, the first man in his unfallen state, which says that he had angels for his servants, that he had power and authority to command them to minister to his needs. Perhaps this is true. But we do know it is true of the second man, the last Adam, our blessed Lord. Angels were His ministers.

In Judges 13:8-9, we find a very interesting passage of Scripture concerning the angelic announcement of the birth of Samson. I am including the passage here because it so closely parallels the statement Jesus made concerning His authority to request angels. "Then Manoah intreated the Lord, and said, O my Lord, let the man of God which thou didst send come again unto us, and teach us what we shall do unto the child that shall be born. And God hearkened to the voice of Manoah;

and the angel of God came again unto the woman as she sat in the field."

Here we find that God sent an angel to Manoah in answer to his specific request. This Scripture is very clear and leaves no room for doubt. This is an Old Testament Scripture. In the New Testament we found Jesus had the authority to specifically request the service of angels.

Additional Scriptures where angels came in answer to prayer can be found in the New Testament. For instance, during the time of the Early Church, when Herod cast Peter into prison, the Church prayed for him without ceasing. God sent an angel to deliver Peter. The answer was so quick and astonishing that those praying were startled. They could hardly believe it was Peter standing at the door of their prayer room, while they were still praying for his deliverance. In fact, they thought it was Peter's angel rather than Peter (Acts 12:1-17).

In John's vision into heaven, he saw an angel attending the altar of incense (Rev. 8:2-4).

In the Old Testament, a priest saw the same angel in the tabernacle (Exod. 30:1-10). The angel was given incense to offer with the prayers of the saints. When the angel placed the incense upon the live coals on the altar, smoke ascended with the prayers of the saints before the throne of God. The angel then took coals in his censer and cast them to earth, as if to prelude coming judgment.

Apparently, people were praying for God to judge the wicked world. These prayers were answered when the angel brought them before God and the seven angels sounded their judgment on earth.

In the New Testament accounts of angels listed above, angelic intervention came in answer to prayer.

Since we have found Scriptures in both the Old and New Testaments in which individuals displayed the authority to request the service of angels, then our requirements of proof according to the rules of interpretation of legal documents have been fully satisfied. In addition, it has been clearly stated in both the Old and New Testaments that angels are God's messengers whose purpose is to minister for His people.

Notice carefully the wording used in Hebrews 1:14. It says angels minister for the believer and not to the believer. The wording used in legal documents is of great importance. Every word must be carefully considered when attempting to understand the meaning the writer had in mind.

The word *for* here is important because it conveys with it an understanding of supervision or control. If the word *to* were used, there would be no control or supervision implied.

There are a great many references to angels ministering for and delivering believers in the New Testament. But we will cover many of these in later chapters. Suffice it to say here that it has been legally established beyond reasonable doubt that it is the covenant right of the believer to expect the ministry of God's angels in his behalf. The believer would also be well within his legal, new covenant right to specifically request of God the assistance of angels, as did Jesus in the New Testament and Manoah, Abraham, and Daniel in the Old Testament.

[1] A.C. Gaebelein, *What the Bible Says About Angels* (Grand Rapids, MI: Baker Book House, 1975).

Chapter 14

Worshiping with Angels

As I studied the Scriptures concerning angels, I found one of their primary ministries is worshiping and praising God. Isaiah's awesome vision of the throne of God included seraphim on either side of the throne singing praises to Jehovah.

We read in Isaiah 6:1-3: "In the year that King Uzziah died I saw also the Lord sitting upon a throne, high and lifted up, and his train filled the temple. Above it stood the seraphims: each one had six wings; with twain he covered his face, and with twain he covered his feet, and with twain he did fly. And one cried unto another and said, Holy, holy, holy, is the Lord of hosts; the whole earth is full of his glory."

Again, in Revelation 4:6-11 we see angels around the throne singing praises and worship to God. A ministry of praise and worship to God is also ascribed to angels in the following Scriptures: Revelation 5:8-13; Job 38:7; and various other scriptures, especially the Psalms.

In this chapter we will be concerned more with angels worshiping God in church services with the believer and ministering for the believer rather than their heavenly worship of God.

There have been many experiences reported where angels were seen by believers during a church service. As someone said to me during my interview with them concerning an angel they had seen in church, "Do you suppose your guardian angel stays home to watch television while you are in church? I should hope the angels are in church with us." I suppose this could be one explanation as to why angels are often seen in church services.

During the year 1960 I had two very unusual experiences with angels while in a church service. Both of these occurred at Sabine Tabernacle in Beaumont, Texas, where the late Harry H. Hodge was pastor. Pastor Hodge always held a Sunday afternoon praise and worship service and I usually attended.

I remember arriving a little late one Sunday afternoon, after the singing was in full swing. As I approached the front door from the street, I could hear what sounded like the voices of thousands of people singing in one accord, as if only one person was singing. After the choruses, the congregation began praising God, and their voices echoed like rolling thunder throughout the gigantic old auditorium. They sang all in one accord as if they were only one great voice. "Hallelujah, Hallelujah, glory, glory to God. Hallelujah," their praises filled the auditorium.

I felt the mighty presence of God the instant I walked into the church. As the audience worshiped and praised God by singing choruses and clapping their hands, I suddenly began experiencing the power of God in my hands so that my hands clapped in perfect time to the music without my consciously moving them. I just held out my hands and they moved under the influence of the power of God. Several others I talked with after the meeting had the same experience.

Then, Pastor Hodge announced that he had seen an angel standing near the front of the auditorium just below the platform. The angel said, "I have troubled the waters for a special blessing."

The musicians began playing "Come and Dine, the Master Calleth," with Pastor Hodge playing his tambourine. Suddenly, a group of men jumped from their seats and ran toward the front of the auditorium, and began "dancing in the Spirit" in perfect rhythm to the music. Soon a great many others joined them.

I remained in my seat, although, I wanted desperately to join the others at the front of the church. I had never before experienced such a thing and I was embarrassed. The men were dancing in perfect step to the music and I felt I would make a fool of myself if I went up front and walked around. I was sure that I could not dance as they were doing.

On sudden impulse I overcame fear, jumped to my feet, and walked hurriedly to join the others who were having such a great time praising and worshiping

God in the dance. The men were dancing in a circular motion in front of the platform. I had walked only a few steps, trying to keep out of the way, when the power of God hit me. My feet began to move in a dance in perfect rhythm to the music.

We had danced for some five minutes when I observed that I was unable to clearly see the men across the auditorium from me. A white misty cloud had settled over the front of the auditorium. I felt my skin tingle as if touched by an electrical current.

Some of the men fell under the power of God. The others stood in a semicircle around the platform praising God. Observing the men next to me, I noted that their faces radiated the glory of God. I thought of the Scripture in the Bible where it said the glory of God was upon Moses and his face so shined with the glory of God that he was forced to cover his face with a cloth, because the people could not look upon him.

After the men had danced, some of the women began dancing in the same way. Toward the end of the service Harry Hodge said that the Lord had reminded him of the Scripture where an angel once a year came and troubled the waters at the pool Bethesda so that God's power was there to heal. It was later discovered that several people did receive miraculous healings while the power of God was strongly present.

On another occasion during the same year at the Sabine Tabernacle, I again attended a very unusual service where an angel was seen. Pastor Hodge had recently received a visitation from the Holy Spirit concerning his ministry. He related the following story that afternoon.

During the night the Holy Spirit came over him in the form of a blanket as he lay in bed. The Holy spirit cried out through Harry's own voice, "THIS IS YOUR MINISTRY FOR THE END TIME."

After the morning service the next day (they held services every morning and evening), a lady came to the front of the auditorium for prayer. Pastor Hodge stepped down to pray for her and then, on sudden impulse from the Holy Spirit, took the jacket which was draped over her shoulder and laid it across her right shoulder.

Immediately the power of God came upon the lady and she fell to the floor. She arose within a few minutes and took the jacket and swung it several times toward the floor. A wave of the glory of God moved through the audience. Others came to the front to receive ministry.

The pastor laid the jacket across each one's shoulder and the power of God came upon them in the same way.

During the service that night, others came forth to receive ministry with no invitation being given. Since he had returned the lady's jacket, Harry Hodge removed the huge cloth from his pulpit and used it to minister to the people. Again, each one received a manifestation of the power of God similar to that experienced by those ministered to that morning.

As the pastor was praying that night, asking God to show him a scriptural precedent for this unusual experience, God reminded him of Elijah's mantle and the cloths which Paul sent out.

On that Sunday afternoon after service, Pastor Hodge offered ministry of the mantle. He said God had shown him it was indeed a special anointing for the end time. A good number of people walked upon the platform and waited their turn. He ministered only to those the Spirit pointed out to him.

After several had been ministered to, a man stood in the audience and announced he had just seen an angel standing beside Harry Hodge. The angel touched each one as they received the ministry of the mantle.

At first I felt apprehensive over this strange ministry. Trying to keep an open mind, I quickly looked up the Scriptures Harry Hodge had quoted.

I had known Harry Hodge for a good number of years and knew him to be a very logical and business type person. I felt I could trust his judgment. The Scriptures were certainly there, in both the Old and New Testament, in which a piece of cloth was used in ministry.

I sat back in the audience and observed the ministry for awhile. I then felt impressed of the Lord to go to receive the ministry. With still some reluctance, but in obedience, I walked to the platform. I stood among the others for awhile.

Harry Hodge then looked directly at me. Immediately, when he looked at me and before he said anything, I felt the power of God move over my body.

"You've been hanging around here for a long time, young man. You've been looking for something haven't you?" he asked. "Well, God has something special for you."

With that he laid the mantle across my shoulder. I completely blanked out. The next thing I remembered I was waving the mantle in front of me and dancing in the Spirit.

I was told later that I had fallen on my back the instant the mantle touched me. I had then gotten up and shouted praises to God while dancing in the Spirit and waving the mantle.

For several days after receiving this unusual ministry, the power of God was resident in my body. I was speaking in a church on the following Wednesday, and when people came for prayer after the service, the power of God was manifested in a very unusual way. When the anointing came upon me to pray for the sick, everyone who touched me, or just brushed up against my body, fell under the power of God.

I relate these experiences in considerable detail because I believe strongly that we are going to experience the moving of God in some unusual, but certainly scriptural, ways in coming days. We must remain open-minded and carefully follow the leadership of the Holy Spirit in our services. It is very easy to miss God's best when a rigid program is closely followed meeting after meeting.

There is nothing as refreshing as a mighty outpouring of the Holy Spirit during a church service. I have learned that God may at times send special angels to assist in bringing this about. There is much evidence to this effect.

An unusual anointing of the Holy Spirit occurred during the first services held in the new First Baptist Church auditorium in Houston. John Roberts related the following experience.

On Sunday morning April 3, 1977, John was seated near the front of the huge auditorium enjoying the beautiful singing of the choir. He was thinking that the choir sounded especially anointed that morning when he noticed a movement above the back row of the choir. He looked closely at the area of movement. A row of angels stood above the choir and all along the brick wall and curtains behind the choir.

John described the angels as very tall, perhaps eight feet or more. They wore white robes made of a material which had the appearance of homespun linen. The angels appeared to have white hair, or at least their hair was light in color.

There is another very interesting aspect of this appearance of the angels. J.C. Spencer, a deacon in the church, had researched the time of the resurrection of Christ and had found it to be on April 3, at around 11 a.m. J.C. had given this information to Pastor John Bisagno the night before the service.

Pastor John Bisagno's sermon that morning was entitled "Christ Is Risen." Those I interviewed reported that Brother Bisagno ministered under a tremendous anointing of the Holy Spirit. Perhaps the angels brought a special blessing to the service. And, then, maybe, it was the Father's way of celebrating the anniversary of the resurrection of His Son!

Evangelist Roxanne Brant reports a very intriguing experience with an angel in one of her services. She was conducting a revival in a Methodist church near Syracuse, New York. Roxanne had her own organist but after the first night discovered that it would require more than a talented musician to get music from the organ in that church.

Chuck, her organist, searched the next day in the community for an organ that could be rented, but found none.

Roxanne prayed for God to somehow help them to get more sound from the old organ. That night in church she was in for a great surprise. It sounded like they had a brand new organ. The whole congregation joined in the praise and worship service with tremendous anointing and enthusiasm. Then, the power of God moved into the auditorium and seemed to literally fall on the congregation.

The Spirit of God fell so heavily that everything just stopped; the music, the singing, everything. Roxanne said you could hear a pin drop. A holy hush fell over the audience. People began falling on their knees between the pews. Roxanne remembers smelling a sweet incense.

Suddenly, while standing behind the pulpit wondering what was happening, God opened Roxanne's eyes so that she could see into the Spirit realm. Standing directly in front of her was a huge muscular angel who looked to be about ten feet tall. He had white hair and wore a white robe. Rippling and bulging muscles could be seen beneath the robe. On the robe was embroidered a golden Greek key design. The angel was facing the audience and only his back and shoulders were visible to Roxanne. She saw the angel for only a few seconds.

When she saw the angel, the Spirit of the Lord revealed to her that the angel's presence was the reason for the intensity of the power of God.

People continued singing and worshiping God, and the power of God fell on various individuals in the audience. Many were healed as they stood in the audience and great numbers came for salvation.

Just as Roxanne was going to dismiss the service, a man spoke up and said he had heard angels singing in the service. She asked how many had heard the angels and had smelled the incense. Nearly every hand was raised. In fact, she said that people in the area are still talking about the night they heard the angels sing.

Our friends in Houston, Charles and Francis Hunter, have also experienced the ministry of angels in their services. One appearance of the angels was during a seminar in Abilene. The ministry of angels was revealed to Rev. W. Estes, pastor of an Assembly of God church in Abilene. Rev. W. Estes was attending the seminar on a Saturday morning when he looked up and saw a band of angels across the top of the Civic Auditorium directly in front of the curtain over the stage. Directly behind this row of angels was another row of angels.

The first group of angels was flying and was much smaller than the second group. The second group carried swords and shields.

The Lord spoke to Pastor Estes concerning the angels. The first group was flying angels bringing a blessing to the people. The second group was called warrior angels, sent to defeat the religious spirit in Abilene which was binding God's people.

The Hunters report another occurrence of angels in their meetings. Toward the end of a service they were holding in California, when the altar call was given the first angel appeared. He was a flying angel and appeared to be blowing a horn. Immediately following the flying angel were many other angels, each carrying a set of tongs and a bucket of coals of fire.

The angels gathered around the front where people were being ministered to. When Francis touched someone and ministered to them, an angel placed a coal of fire in that person's mouth.

The one ministered to would fall under the power of God and begin speaking in other tongues. One boy in particular had just been saved and knew nothing of the baptism in the Holy Spirit. But when the angel placed that hot coal in his mouth, he fell and began speaking in a heavenly language.

Immediately after the angels had deposited their coals they left the service. Some of the people ministered to reported a sensation on their lips, as if they had been hit in the mouth.

There are many other reports of angels ministering in church services, far too many to include them all. However, we may conclude that angels certainly have a part in our worship services, and at times their ministry seems to be connected with a special out-pouring of the Holy Spirit on the service.

Also, it is interesting to note how the reports on the sightings of angels concur. Flying angels were seen by different people in other places, and each time they were reported as smaller than the other angels. The general appearance of the larger angels was described in the same way each time they were sighted. We will see in later chapters how closely the report of blessing and warrior angels concur with the Scriptures.

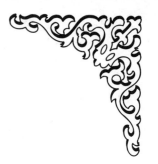

Chapter 15

Throne Room Experiences

Both John and the prophet Isaiah describe some awesome yet thrilling experiences in which their spirits left their bodies and ascended before the throne of God. In Revelation 4:2 John gives a very similar description to what Isaiah experienced (Isa. 6:1-3).

The prophet Micaiah received a prophecy in the form of a vision for the King of Israel, Ahab, in which he saw God seated on a throne surrounded by angelic creatures. "I saw the Lord sitting on his throne, and all the host of heaven standing by him on his right and on his left" (1 Kings 22:19).

In all three instances, there were angels present, each apparently with specific ministries. Also, all three men saw God the Father seated on His throne.

In 2 Kings 19:14-15 we find a reference to a cherubim located below the throne. Here we read: "And Hezekiah received the letter of the hand of the messengers, and read it: and Hezekiah went up into the house of the Lord, and spread it before the Lord. And Hezekiah prayed before the Lord, and said, O Lord God of Israel, which dwellest between the cherubims, thou art the God, even thou alone, of all the kingdom of the earth; thou hast made heaven and earth."

A more correct translation says the throne was located above the cherubims rather than between the cherubims. In 1 Samuel 4:4, Psalm 80:1, and Psalm 99:1 a reference is made to the throne of God being located above the cherubims.

Only one reference in the Bible is made of the other type of angelic creature, the six-winged seraphim. This mention of the seraphim is found in Isaiah 6:2, which has been previously mentioned at the beginning of this chapter.

In all probability, the seraphim and cherubim have heavenly ministries that differ decidedly from the ministering spirits assigned to minister for the heirs of salvation. Possibly, the cherubim is the highest type of an angelic creature and their ministry seems to be concerned with guarding the throne of God and acting as God's ambassadors. On the other hand, the seraphim is apparently more involved in the worship of God and the leadership of his servants in worship.

In April 1960 I received a vision in which my spirit left my body and ascended to the throne. This experience occurred not long after I had received the ministry of the mantle described in a previous chapter.

I had been fasting and praying for several days prior to the vision. After coming in from church on a Sunday night, I changed clothes and walked around in the yard praying for an hour or so before retiring. This was my habit of prayer at night so that I would not disturb my parents, since I was living at home at the time.

After going to bed, I lay quietly for awhile and meditated on the Word of God. Within a few minutes I felt a strange sensation, as if I could not move my limbs. Then I discovered that I could not move my limbs nor speak; the thought came to me that I was dying. I knew no fear, nor did I struggle. I knew that I was prepared to die, though not ready to die just yet. However, if it were God's time, I would accept it.

All feeling left my body and my spirit ascended up through the roof. I found myself standing on some very bright steps which inclined at about a 30-degree angle. As far as I could see there were steps. The steps were bright, but in front and above me there was a brightness so great that I could not look directly at it.

Then as I stood on the steps, I heard a voice like thunder coming from the direction of the intense brightness. The instant the voice spoke I felt myself melt so that it seemed that I was nothing but a tiny spot on the steps. And when the voice began to speak, I could make no reply. Every thought was drained from my mind. I could hear the voice but I could not reply.

I know I heard the voice of God the Father. I have never heard a voice like that before or since. And certainly there is no voice like it to compare.

The father spoke to me quite at length concerning the ministry He had for me. He described the end-time revival we are now beginning to experience and told me that there would be raised up prophets with great power like the prophets in the Old Testament during this last revival which will be experienced worldwide.

Most of the things he spoke about were of a personal nature concerning the commission He had for me. However, He did mention the ministry of angels and said that His angels would protect and keep me.

I do not know how long I stood on the steps. But, immediately after the Father had finished talking with me, my spirit again entered my body and the normal senses returned. I could move and speak, as though nothing had happened. I was in a state of semi-shock for a few seconds, and then I began praising God for the great and awesome vision He had given me.

A few months later I had a similar experience. It was during a Sunday night service in my home church, Glad Tidings Assembly of God, in Beaumont, Texas, where Rev. Jack Fellars was pastor.

A visiting evangelist was ministering that night. He had just gotten up to the pulpit to begin speaking when someone gave a message in tongues. I felt a strong urge to stand to my feet and begin speaking, although I had never given an interpretation to a message in tongues.

I waited awhile and when no one gave the interpretation, I began speaking out the interpretation under a heavy anointing. The power of God moved into the service and people began running to the altar. Some fell in the aisles before they reached the altars.

I, too, ran to the front of the church and fell across an altar. I had no more than touched the altar when my spirit left my body and I found myself kneeling on the same steps I had been standing on a few months prior. However, I did not hear God Almighty's voice as before. But I did hear the most beautiful singing, worshiping, and praising of God I have ever heard. I heard the voices of thousands of God's heavenly creatures, the angels, singing praises to God. How long I was on those throne steps I do not know. But it must have been for quite some time.

When my spirit came into my body again, Brother Casey Jones and another brother in the church were praying for me. Although they didn't say it, they acted and looked like they thought I had died and returned to life.

Chapter 16

Angels — Agents of Healing

Few of us have ever thought of angels as being used in physical healing for our bodies. Yet, it is mentioned in the Scriptures. For example, we read John 5:4, "For an angel went down at a certain season into a pool, and troubled the water: whosoever then first after the troubling of the water stepped in was made whole of whatsoever disease he had."

Of course, as Bible scholars will point out, some translations do not include verse four of the fifth chapter of John. However, the King James Version does include the fourth verse so we reference it here.

We will not attempt to explain why God chose to use an angel as an agent of healing at the Pool of Bethesda. But suffice it to say that here we have discovered another instance where angels were used in bringing about healing.

Another New Testament reference to angels used in bringing physical strength or healing is found in Matthew 4:11. Here we read: "Then the devil leaveth him, and, behold, angels came and ministered unto him."

After Jesus had been fasting for 40 days and enduring strong conflict from Satan, God sent His angels to bring strength and healing to the spirit, mind, and body of Jesus.

Again, when Jesus was agonizing in the Garden of Gethsemane, just before His terrible but blessed death on the Cross, an angel appeared to strengthen Him. At that climactic night in the history of the world, every demon of hell, every angel of Satan, was summoned to insure that Jesus was put to death. All of hell rejoiced that night.

The Bible says that Jesus agonized under such pressure that great drops of blood came through His skin and rolled down His face. All physical, mental, and spiritual strength had ebbed away. But God sent an angel to bring healing in all three areas — spirit, mind, and body. "And there appeared an angel unto him from heaven, strengthening him" (Luke 22:43).

In the Old Testament there are several dramatic illustrations of angels ministering to men to bring strength and healing. One example, the time where Prophet Elijah was ministered to and fed by an angel, has already been mentioned in a previous chapter. Let's look at one other instance where healing and strength came as a result of God's angels.

We read in Daniel 10:8, "Therefore I was left alone, and saw this great vision, and there remained no strength in me: for my comeliness was turned in me into corruption, and I retained no strength."

And Daniel 10:16 continues, "And, behold, one like the similitude of the sons of men touched my lips: then I opened my mouth, and spake, and said unto him that stood before me, O my lord, by the vision my sorrows are turned upon me, and I have retained no strength." In Daniel 10:18 we are told the angel brought strength and physical healing.

The stories related in this chapter concerning God's use of angels in healing are all examples of God's miracle power working in our behalf. Jesus is the healer of the New Testament believer. But He is free to use whatever agent or instrument He so desires to bring about our healing.

Jesus is the healer and we should not look to angels for our healing. On the other hand, we never know how many healings may be the result of God sending His ministering spirits to strengthen us and we are not aware of it.

Since the angels do minister strength, I do not believe we are out of line with the Word of God by asking the Father in the name of Jesus to send an angel to minister to us in times of dire need. Once, when I was on the 22nd day of a fast, I found myself in a position where I needed physical strength.

I was in the area of our farm attending to some business, and stopped by the farm to pray and relax. However, a man I employed to plow a hay meadow was there and informed me he was ready to plant the grass seed. I had not expected him to plow until sometime later when I had finished my fast.

However, the seedbed had been prepared and he needed for me to purchase the seed, then walk over the ten-acre field and spread the seed with a hand broadcasting unit while he came behind me with the tractor and covered the seed. My physical strength was at a low ebb. I had already exerted myself by driving to an area and conducting some minor business. It was June and the day very warm.

What was I to do? I didn't feel that I could tell a man who wasn't a Christian that I was on a religious fast and, therefore, couldn't work just now. That would require that he go to the trouble and expense of bringing his tractor back again, and would also mean reworking the seedbed if it rained significantly before I returned.

I felt it would be better to inform the man that although I was on a religious fast, God would supply me sufficient strength to complete the job. I prayed and asked the Father in the name of Jesus to send an angel to minister strength to me. I remembered that Elijah was ministered to by an angel.

I bought 200 pounds of grass seed, marked off the planting with sticks so I would walk a straight line, loaded the canvas shoulder bag, and began planting. It was noon and the sun was very hot. Since the man was behind me with the tractor, I had to move at a fast walk to stay ahead.

I had no more than made the first row, when I felt the supernatural strength of God take over. Planting that ten-acre field in the hot sun was the easiest work I had ever done. I felt like superman as I almost ran up and down the rows, turning the crank as fast as I could, and staying way ahead of the tractor.

God had answered my prayer and sent His ministering angels to give me supernatural strength. I was not even tired or sweating when I finished the work.

Another time when God used an angel to administer His healing power was in the fall of 1966 while ministering in Lake Forest Assembly of God Church in Houston, Texas.

After the meeting on a Sunday morning, Leon Spruill came for prayer. I did not know Leon, and had no idea what was wrong with him.

As the pastor, Jolly Terry, and I laid hands on Leon, we prayed that God would kill the roots of the cancer in the lungs. Of course, Leon Spruill was surprised, as he knew I had no knowledge of what was wrong with him.

He went to the hospital the next day and was scheduled to have surgery on Tuesday. On Monday night while lying on his hospital bed praying, he saw an angelic form enter the room and begin writing on the wall. Leon said the form of the angel was bright and flowing but not real clear. However, the hand that wrote on the wall and the writing were brightly illuminated and very distinct. The hand wrote, "I am the Lord that healeth thee."

He slept peacefully the remainder of the night and experienced no fear when he went into the operating room the next day. The doctors were very surprised to find that all the roots of the cancer they removed were dead.

This is another example of God's healing power in which an angel played a part in the healing. But whether or not we are healed by an angel, all healing comes from Jesus the healer. And healing is definitely for the New Testament believer.

Chapter 17

Angels, One of God's Cures for Loneliness

Loneliness has been proclaimed by psychologists as America's number one problem, not only among the elderly, but among all ages. Youth in our time have especially been affected by problems resulting from loneliness and rejection by groups and peers. Loneliness has been a major cause of the recent surge in alcoholism, drug addiction, and homosexuality according to leading authorities.

Of course, Jesus Christ is the answer to all these problems. However, as we have ministered in seminars on the subject of angels, we have discovered a surprisingly large number of Christians are suffering from loneliness and the fear of being alone.

Many Christians suffering from loneliness have come to us after a message on angels to express their appreciation. It was extremely comforting for them to learn they are not alone after all. God's angel is constantly with them to insure that no harm comes to them.

Psalm 34:7 tells us, "The angel of the Lord encampeth round about them that fear him, and delivereth them." This Psalm conveys real comfort to anyone who, of necessity, must live alone. God's angel actually takes up his dwelling around us. Wherever we go our angel is there with us.

Another very revealing message concerning the ministry of angels for the believer is brought forth in the beautiful Psalm 91. Here the Psalmist boldly declares in verses 9-11, "Because thou hast made the Lord, which is my refuge, even the most High, thy habitation; there shall no evil befall thee, neither shall any plague come nigh thy dwelling. For he shall give his angels charge over thee, to keep thee in all thy ways. They shall bear thee up in their hands, lest thou dash thy foot against a stone."

Here is excellent news for those who are living alone. God is so concerned about us that He has given His angels special charge over us. The angels will keep us in all our ways, or wherever we may go.

In 1 Kings 19 there is the story of a very lonely man who had allowed himself to fall into deep depression and despair. The mighty prophet Elijah faced such despair that he ran into the wilderness and asked God to take his life. He felt so alone he considered himself to be the only godly man remaining in all of Israel.

In this very touching story, God sent His angel to care for a man who was too far gone in loneliness and emotional depression to even take care of himself. He had lost the desire to live. However, the angel fed him and provided care and strength.

What a blessing and comfort it is to know that though we are forced at times to walk alone through this life, we are not alone because God is with us and His holy angels minister to our needs and are ever present to protect us.

Once when I was ministering in a foreign country and forced to live alone for awhile, I returned to my hotel room one night completely exhausted and terribly lonely for my family. As I lay upon my bed, I fell into depression. I felt so very alone among so many people who could not speak my language. I called upon the Father and asked Him to help me. I was beyond helping myself. I had lost my appetite and my body was weak.

The Father spoke to me ever so sweetly and said, "I am your family and you are not alone. My ministering spirits are with you even now to bring strength and comfort. Let them work for you."

Almost immediately the depression and loneliness subsided and a real deep settled peace and joy came over me. Physical strength returned to my body, although I had eaten very little in several days. Thank God for His angels who are ever present in the time of need!

An elderly lady who had previously heard our teaching on angels gave us a very interesting report after a meeting one night. Since her husband's death she had remained in their old home which was in a deteriorating neighborhood. Never having learned to drive, she was dependent on her daughter or a friend to drive her to the nearby shopping center. When no one was available it was necessary for her walk through a particularly bad area to reach the grocery store.

One evening when she discovered she was out of a certain needed item and there was no one home to assist her, she began the walk to the store, hoping to return before dark. However, because the store was unusually crowded, it became quite dark before her return.

About halfway home, as she walked near the slum area of vacant buildings, she heard several footsteps behind her. She stood still for several seconds, literally frozen in fear. She didn't know whether to try to make it or to scream for help.

Suddenly, she remembered the angels in the 91st Psalm. She continued walking toward home, raised her one hand which was free of the grocery bag, and began praising God and thanking Him for His angel that walked right beside her.

Then she heard footsteps running on the sidewalk. She thought whoever it was had departed. To her surprise, when she approached an alley between vacant buildings, three young hoodlums walked toward her. From across the street a streetlight illuminated the area enough for her to see that each boy carried either a knife or club. But she had been praising God so intently that she had no doubt God's angel was with her. She knew only peace and experienced no fear.

"Good evening, boys. Do you know Jesus loves you and died for you?" she greeted the three hoodlums.

The boys stood in the alley staring after her for a few seconds. They dropped their knives, sticks, and whatever else they were carrying and ran up the street as if they had seen a ghost.

No doubt they had seen one of God's angels standing with flaming sword beside the lady.

A very moving and heartwarming story is told to us by Beverly Colvin, of God sending one of his angels to bring comfort to a lonely child who was stricken over the loss of a sister.

The year Beverly was four and sister Sissie Sue was five, they were inseparable companions. They played together constantly, sharing dolls and other toys without the usual quarrels of young children.

They ate together and slept together, and one would never leave the other to go with a parent visiting or on an errand unless forced to do so.

Immediately after breakfast, during the warm months of spring and summer, hand-in-hand they trotted, small child fashion, to their favorite play area beneath a giant sprawling oak which grew near the river in front of their Arkansas home. The sand was soft and cool there, and excellent for making playhouses and all other dream castles imaginable.

Then one day in early fall, just as the tree leaves were beginning to turn the hillsides into flaming torches of beauty, little Sissie Sue became ill. Within a short time Sissie Sue went to be with Jesus, Beverly was told by her mother, Lillian Colvin.

For months Beverly went through the house calling for Sissie Sue. After breakfast she hurried to their favorite play area, each day hoping that somehow Sissie Sue would be there.

Beverly was having difficulty sleeping at night, she ate very little, and she cried a lot for her sister. Beverly's mother prayed and sought the Lord earnestly for help. Beverly's constant search and calling for Sissie Sue compounded her mother's grief.

One day little Sissie Sue returned to Beverly at their favorite play area. They played together for an entire afternoon. Later in the day, when Beverly awoke from her nap she explained to her mother how she had played with Sissie Sue and how happy Sissie Sue was in her new home.

From that glorious afternoon until now, Beverly never asked for Sissie Sue again. Since Beverly was so young at the time, she doesn't remember what they talked about or why she was comforted. But in later years when telling the story, she knew with a certainty it was an angel with whom she played that day. An angel that brought healing in such a measure that never again did she go in search of Sissie Sue. Truly, there is help in God alone.

Missionary Arthur F. Berg gives a tremendously inspiring testimony of angels bringing comfort and solace in answer to a lonely and despairing man's prayer in the following story.[1]

I was not dreaming. I did not have a vision. I was wide awake that day, when suddenly the room was filled with the sound of singing voices and music blending in beautiful harmony. Where was it coming from? How? Why?

We were alone on a pioneer mission station at Masisi-Rutchuru in the Kivu District of the Congo. For many days my wife and our little daughter Agnes had been ill with the deadly malaria fever. After holding for several days at 104 degrees, Mrs. Berg's temperature rose to 105.2 degrees. In her weakness, her voice was but a faint whisper, and at times she seemed to be drifting into a semi-coma. I knew her condition was critical, so I called in a group of Congolese Christians to pray with me. They readily responded and prayed earnestly. I was touched by their faith and loyalty, yet the feeling of depression did not leave. Oh, if I only had a fellow missionary!

After awhile I stepped out of our humble thatched-roof home into the African night. It was one of those clear tropical moonlit nights with myriads of stars seemingly suspended from the heavens. They looked so near, as if one could just reach up and touch them.

I looked toward the northeast — our home in the United States, 10,000 miles away. "Oh, God," I prayed, "does anyone at home know our predicament? Does anyone care?"

Years later, after returning to America, I got the answer. A little lady in Minneapolis, a friend of our family, asked me, "Were you and Anna in special need at this certain time in the Congo?"

Then she continued, "I saw your face before me. I was seized with a tremendous burden. I went to God in prayer and prayed till peace and assurance of His answer filled my heart."

We compared dates and learned it was the exact time when I was out in the night, praying and crying to God from a breaking heart.

But on that dark night I knew nothing of this. I went back into the house where the African Christians were still faithfully praying. I urged them to continue while I sat down by our little folding pump organ and began to play. Opening a hymnbook I saw the song, "Was There Ever a Friend So True." It was not a familiar song, but as I sang it the words seemed directed to me. One verse reads:

> He soothes me in sorrow with songs in the night,
> And inspires me with hope anew;
> He fills me with courage my battles to fight,
> Was there ever a friend so true?

I needed the Lord's assurance in that hour. I sang on and on, pouring out my soul to God in the words of the song.

Suddenly the room seemed filled with indescribable music. I was no longer alone! I was aware of a divine presence. A choir, the beauty of which I had never heard before or since, was singing. They were singing of Christ, a friend who was near. For a moment I was startled. I looked around. The Congolese Christians were still in prayer, and then I remembered that they could not sing in English. I turned back to the organ and joined with the invisible choir in singing glory and praise to God. My heart was lifted up and I knew the Lord was very near.

This rapturous moment was interrupted as a door flung open and someone called excitedly, "Madamu, anakufa, Maduma, anakufa!" ("Madam is dying! Madam is dying!") A houseboy who had been watching in the sickroom was standing before me, fear and grief mingled in his face.

Urging the Christians to continue in prayer, I went quickly to my wife. Instead of finding her dying. I saw and heard her praising God, speaking in tongues with a clear and steady voice. Her hands were lifted up in worship and adoration to our wonderful Lord. I knelt and joined with her in thanks to God. I then felt her forehead and found it wet with perspiration. The fever had broken. As we continued to praise God together, her temperature continued to come down.

Later Anna said that in the midst of her suffering it had seemed a ball of fire touched her head and went through her entire body. Its warmth was greater, but so different from the burning fever. The Lord's presence filled her heart, and praises to God naturally followed. God had touched and healed her, and from that moment she regained strength. At the same time our little daughter was also healed.

It had all taken place simultaneously. When I was out in the yard praying, when the African Christians were interceding, and when the little lady in Minnesota also prayed, the answer came. A choir of angels was sent to strengthen a weary missionary with their heavenly singing!

[1] *Pentecostal Evangel* (Springfield, MO: Gospel Publishing House, 1966). Used by permission.

Chapter 18

Angels at Death

Recently there has been much concern over death. Books are being written about the experiences of those who have been clinically dead and then returned to this earth. In hospitals special courses are conducted for the terminally ill, showing them how to better prepare for death. Classes are also held for the relatives so they will be better equipped to make the last days as pleasant as possible.

Concerning the reporting of the experiences of those who have been clinically dead, I was at first surprised that reports have all been good from those who could remember where they had been. But there is a simple explanation. The human mind tends to quickly forget horrifying experiences. Naturally, the mind would quickly shut out any remembrance of something as terrifying as Hell. Unless, of course, God allowed the experience to be remembered by someone who later became a Christian.

Such is the case with Rev. Tom Williams, whose testimony we heard recently.

In 1924, while working near the logging camps in Oregon, Tom fell 35 feet, head first, and struck a steel pipe. He then fell another 20 feet into a 12-foot tank of water.

He lay in the bottom of the tank with a crushed skull and rib-punctured lung for over an hour. Doctors found no water in his lungs when he was pulled from the water. Evidently he had been dead when he entered the water.

A nearby Christian friend was notified of his death. She knelt by his side and prayed that God would raise him from the dead. In fact, she boldly told God that she refused to let Tom die in the unsaved condition he was in because she had spent too many hours in prayer for his salvation.

Tom had already been covered over with a sheet, and his body was ready to be taken to the morgue. The attending doctor was just about to ask that the praying lady be dragged away from the scene, as he thought she must be in shock, when Tom spoke and removed the sheet from his face.

The lady praised God rather loudly and the doctor needed a doctor. The doctor became saved on the spot. He knew there had to be a God when he saw the dead man return to life.

The last thing Tom remembered was falling from the trestle. When he came to he was standing on a cliff overlooking an ocean of fire. As far as he could see in any direction there were rolling billows of blue, orange, and yellow flames of fire.

Out of the fire he saw his uncle and a pal approach him. The uncle had been dead seven years and the friend three years. The flames came halfway between their ankles and knees.

Tom had instant knowledge when he entered the area of the great ocean of fire and seemed to immediately know all things. He knew he was in hell, and a feeling of despair overcame him.

Tom communicated with the uncle and friend by thought transference rather than by speech. The one being communicated to knew instantly what was being thought by the other with no words spoken.

Tom looked up and saw Jesus Christ crossing above the great ocean of fire. He thought, *If only I can get Jesus to look at me, He will get me out of here.* Jesus was almost across the abyss and Tom felt a feeling of eternal doom sweep over him.

But just before Jesus disappeared, He looked back at Tom. Instantly Tom was propelled up and out of the abyss. His spirit entered his body as if he were walking through a door. He then heard his friend praying for him. He moved the sheet from over his eyes and spoke to her. Within five days God had begun a complete and miraculous healing in his body.

Needless to say, death for the unsaved can be a horrifying experience. But for the Christian it can be a blessed time indeed.

There are countless reports of those who have seen angels while on their deathbed. The many testimonies of angels at the death of the Christian, coupled with the account in Luke 16:22 of Lazarus being carried by angels to paradise or Abraham's bosom, should be reassuring to any believer. Then, too, I am convinced that our Father prepares us for death when it is nearby, giving us supernatural faith and peace.

My maternal grandmother, Lucille O'Neil, had a very beautiful experience at death. She had been in a tubercular hospital for several years before her death. While there, she prayed with many patients and conducted a regular little counseling center in her room.

I was attending college during most of her stay in the hospital but visited her nearly every weekend without fail. "Nona," as the grandchildren called her, was more like a mother to me than a grandmother.

God began preparing Nona for her homecoming several days before her actual departure. Or, as I have often thought later, perhaps He was just delaying her departure until I was able to visit her one more time and learn from her own lips of her blessed experiences before death.

I was with her on the night before her death. All she talked about that night was the beautiful flowers, the sweet-smelling fragrance of the flowers, and the angel who stood at the pathway leading through the flower garden. Occasionally, the angel waved to her.

And then one night she dreamed she had talked with several of her close friends who had been dead for many years.

"It was as if they were in the room with me," she told me. And also there was the music she had been hearing for several days and nights. Several times she awakened during the night and tried to turn off her radio, thinking that was the source of the beautiful music.

I stayed with her until late in the night. We prayed together and she shared the beautiful scenes of heaven which her spiritual eyes could see but my natural eyes could not. I was the only one with her that last evening.

Once during the night she pointed toward the ceiling of her plain little room and said, "There he [the angel] is now, waving again. He is standing among the most beautiful roses I have ever seen. And there is the darling rock path leading over a brook and through the garden. Can you smell the roses?"

"No," I said, squeezing her hand, "I cannot smell the roses, but I know they are beautiful. They must be just for you."

When she had gone to sleep, I kissed her cheek and went home to sleep for a few hours, thinking I would return to visit with her early the next day. But we received a call the next morning informing us that her heart had stopped beating shortly after I had left.

Nona went home to be with the Lord in April of 1960. I remember it today as if it had been only a few days ago.

My dad, Reverend Alvin French, also had a very beautiful experience in which God prepared him for death. Approximately one month before his death, Dad was visited by an angel during the night. Dad never told us exactly what the angel said, but he did reveal that he had seen some scenes in heaven, including friends and relatives who had been dead for quite some time.

Immediately after the heavenly vision a change came over Dad. He had a faraway look in his eyes, almost a look of nostalgia, as he was visiting friends and relatives. His friends told me later that Dad squeezed their hand before leaving and said goodbye in a way that made them wonder.

Of course, Dad had said very little about the vision and then only to a few close family members. He told no one that the vision meant that he would not be with us much longer.

The last time I saw Dad alive was about three weeks before his death. I asked him if he would like to make a trip to Mexico with me to preach in some of the villages. I thought it strange when he looked away and said he wouldn't be able to make it.

As we were leaving that Sunday afternoon, Dad held my son Keith in his lap and talked to him at length concerning Keith's living his life for Christ and his future. I should have suspected something then, but I didn't. Since we lived over a hundred miles away, I did not return until I received the call announcing his heart attack.

Although I arrived too late to see him alive, I knew the very minute the angel came for him. I was driving the one hundred miles to the hospital, praying for Dad in my heavenly language when suddenly I felt the power of God go through my body so strongly I was nearly lifted from the car seat.

The Spirit said, "That was my resurrecting power, and his angel has just left with him."

I glanced at my watch and later found that it was the exact time of Dad's death. Immediately after the Spirit spoke to me, the burden to pray lifted from me and I experienced a deep-settled peace.

I will always be grateful to my dear friend Rev. B.H. Clendennen, for being with Dad at his death. He said Dad had a real peace and just relaxed and waited for his homecoming.

Death for the believer need not be a frightful experience, but should be a time of rejoicing. This is demonstrated very clearly by the testimony of a very saintly lady who was pronounced clinically dead for over five minutes at Herman Hospital in Houston in 1965.

Sibil Spruill was a member of Lake Forest Assembly of God Church in Houston. She was taken to Herman Hospital for treatment after a severe attack of asthma. She underwent another attack while at the hospital and died as a result of it.

Sister Spruill described her experience at death as something so beautiful and pleasant that there are not sufficient descriptive terms in man's language to aptly relate the reality of heaven. She explained death as passing into a dream-like state where there was no pain or sorrow, and everything became immensely beautiful and pleasant.

She saw white robes on man-like forms, but saw no faces. After being ushered into an atmosphere of brightness and beauty, she eventually came to a resting place which seemed to be a waiting area before entering heaven. The white-robed angels stood on either side of her as she looked upon the breathtaking beauty of the heavenly scenes before her. Everywhere she looked she saw indescribably beautiful flowers, streams, and glowing white structures which appeared to be buildings.

The angelic forms by her side seemed to be discussing whether to take her into the beautiful brightness which stretched before her, or to return her to earth. The same robed angelic forms then lifted her from the place where she was standing and moved swiftly toward earth. An instant later she found her spirit entering her body again, just in the way it had departed, almost as if a vacuum had pulled it into the body.

When she awoke, the attack of asthma had gone, and she later discovered she was completely healed.

The apostle Paul said once that he had difficulty deciding whether it would be better to depart and be with Christ, or to remain on earth. In 2 Corinthians 5:8 he made it clear that he was willing to be absent from the body and to be present with the Lord.

And, of course, Paul was there when Stephen was stoned to death, and he heard Stephen cry out that he saw Jesus standing on the Father's right hand. In Paul's mind there was no doubt, and Paul's spirit longed for a meeting with his Lord.

Chapter 19

Heaven's 24-Hour Emergency Service

It is one of the covenant blessings of the believer to enjoy divine protection from accidents. And just how is this brought about you might wonder? Why, through His ministering spirits, the holy angels, of course.

Psalm 91 is very explicit concerning our protection from accidents. "There shall no evil befall you, nor any plague or calamity come near your tent" (Ps. 91:10;AMP). The word *calamity* here means accident. Then we read further, "For He will give His angels charge over you, to accompany and defend and preserve you in all your ways [of obedience and service]. They shall bear you up on their hands, lest you dash your foot against a stone" (Ps. 91:11-12). Notice the legal wording in verse 11. The word FOR is the connecting word with the preceding sentence. The believer is protected from accidents "for" or because His angels accompany us everywhere we go. The angels are with us 24 hours a day.

These covenant promises are repeated in Luke 4:10-11.

For an illustration from the Bible, let's examine Acts 27:22-24. We find the apostle Paul traveling by ship to Rome. He was going about the King's business. Paul was to be a witness for Jesus Christ in Rome.

A terrible storm threatened the ship and the lives of the 200 men on board. Paul spoke to the terrified men and said, "And now I exhort you to be of good cheer: for there shall be no loss of any man's life among you, but of the ship. For there stood by me this night the angel of God, whose I am, and whom I serve, saying, Fear not, Paul; thou must be brought before Caesar: and, lo, God hath given thee all them that sail with thee" (Acts 27:22-23).

Interesting, isn't it, that an angel was sent to deliver Paul? Well, the Bible said the angels were charged to keep us from calamities or accidents.

Now, let's look at some modern examples of believers rescued by angels. No doubt, though, we are spared from accidents many times during our life and never even know about it. Only eternity will tell. I certainly have a lot of "thank you's" stored up for my angel when I see him in glory.

My friend Johnny Spruill and I were enjoying a good cup of coffee while he was relating the angelic deliverance which follows.

As I was taking notes, Johnny said, "You know I am certainly glad angels don't take coffee breaks or go on vacation or sleep like we humans do. I am glad they are on 24-hour duty."

Johnny is a licensed tankerman and owns a partnership in a business which specializes in loading and unloading petroleum products from barges in the Port of Houston. As Johnny was working one morning in 1970, the Spirit of the Lord spoke to him so vividly that he jumped around, thinking someone had called to him. The Lord said, "Johnny, you shall walk through the valley of the shadow of death. But fear no evil, for I am with you and My angels have charge over you."

At around ten o'clock that night Johnny was very busy trying to unload four barges that had come into port that evening. Only one employee was available to assist him.

There was a high wind and the barges bounced and bucked in the waves. Walking on the barges and jumping from one to the other was especially difficult, but necessary, as the unloading hoses had to be moved across the huge vessels.

Suddenly, just as Johnny stepped out to cross over to the next barge, a wave came up, parting the barges. Johnny fell over 12 feet to the water and went under very deep, deep enough, he thought, to come up under one of the barges rather than between them. Even as he went under and knew the total darkness of the foamy waters between the gigantic steel vessels, he tried desperately to fight back the sickening fear and panic.

Just as he surfaced, popping out of the threatening waters like a monstrous flying fish, he remembered the strange words the Lord spoke that morning, *"Fear no evil! Fear not!"*

Johnny began to praise God for deliverance. On either side of Johnny were barges, looming in the darkness for all the world like giant steel coffins. If the wind blew again, or a ship passed in the channel, the barges would close together — around Johnny. A devastating crush seemed inevitable. As it was, he barely had room to turn sideways in the water. He tried to place his feet on the side of either barge and climb out.

It was no use! He could not grip the slick sides of the steel barges, and the deck was 12 feet straight up. Johnny's assistant was supposed to be two barges over, working around the pump, and above the noise it would be impossible for him to hear a call.

But Johnny began calling with all his might. In his spirit he praised God to keep down the panic and fear. A wind came up and the barges rocked.

Johnny had not called more than four or five times when the assistant answered. A rope ladder was thrown down and Johnny quickly climbed out of the dark death trap.

For no reason that he could think of, the assistant had left his work station and walked over to where Johnny had been working. The barges remained stationary, as if there had been no wind.

God's angels were on duty that night. One held the barges apart while the other summoned the assistant. And, as Johnny said, we can all be glad our angels don't take coffee breaks.

In 1965 when my son Keith was two years old, he met with what could have been a very serious accident. We were packing the car for a trip and Keith followed us in and out of the house.

Apparently, Keith climbed up into the car far enough to reach the gear shift and pull the lever out of "park" position. The driveway was on a slant and the car quickly rolled into the street.

From inside the house we heard Keith's screams and came running. He was lying in the driveway and I could see black marks from the tire tread over his left leg.

We grabbed him up and rushed him to the hospital emergency room, thanking God for deliverance as we went. Before we reached the hospital, Keith had quit crying and he could move his leg with no apparent pain.

After examining the x-rays, the attending physician just shook his head in unbelief. "Little boy, your guardian angel was watching over you," he said to Keith.

Then turning to me, the doctor said, "As long as I have been practicing medicine I have never seen anything like this. The tire marks are on his leg clearly yet there are no broken bones, no breaks in his flesh or even a bruise."

The doctor explained clearly to me what happened. And it was worth every cent he charged for me to find out. You see, I didn't understand the ministry of angels then as I do now. I knew God delivered Keith. But I didn't understand what part the angels played in our protection and deliverance.

But the good doctor gave me a lesson in angelic deliverance and only charged $15 for it. Well, $15 plus x-rays. I've wondered how the doctor knew what happened. Perhaps the Holy Spirit spoke through the doctor to teach me about angels.

Keith and I had a very unusual experience when ministering in Mexico in 1971. We had been ministering in the villages and were on our way back to Texas. We had crossed the last checkpoint some ten miles back when our pickup coughed and sputtered, indicating it was out of gas.

I had not filled up at the last town we had passed, nor had I filled my spare gas cans, as I felt we had sufficient gasoline to reach the border. At that time U.S. gasoline was much lower in price and of better quality than that in Mexico.

I lifted the hood of the truck as a signal for help. I gave myself a good chewing out for being so stupid as to run out of gas in Mexico. There was no traffic on the road, not even a burro. No houses were in sight.

We decided to walk to the top of the hill in front of us to see if we could spot any sign of human life. We had walked no more than a hundred yards when a car with Texas license plates came over the hill and pulled up beside us. It was a young couple on their honeymoon. The groom had noticed a house several miles back and would take us there. If we found no help, he would bring us back to the truck.

We had traveled no more than a mile when we spotted a small vacant-looking shack by the side of the road where fruit was sold in season. Noticing a Mexican man near the small building, the groom stopped.

I walked over to the Mexican man, hoping at least to rent a couple of burros to pull my truck to the border. When I mentioned gas, in Spanish, of course, the little man showed a mouth full of teeth, which looked even whiter against the framing of his dark face.

"Si! Si!" he cried out happily, running toward the shack. Out of the shack he came with two one-gallon glass jars.

On the way back to our truck I was able to witness to the young couple about how Jesus Christ had supplied our needs.

On the way back to the border I would stop at the shack and return the Mexican's glass jars. Glass jars were not easy to come by in the back country.

After we had gone a few miles, I turned around thinking I had passed the shack. We went all the way to where we had run out of gas but never did find the shack to return the bottles. I do not believe we could have missed anything that obvious and so close to the road.

Thinking back on it now, I wish I had kept the bottles and had the glass analyzed. It would be interesting to know the content of glass used in heaven.

Norman Williams, a survivor of the worst air crash in history, tells how God spared his life:

I'm one of the few survivors of the world's worst aircraft disaster. There were 653 passengers on two jumbo jets that collided on Canary Island, March 27, 1977 — 593 were killed and only 60 survived. How I escaped from this fiery crash is nothing short of a miracle.

The day we left Los Angeles my widowed mother, who has lived with me for 18 years, prayed for traveling mercies for me. As she prayed she began to weep, and this startled me because this was the first time I'd ever seen her crying. She was weeping so bitterly, she couldn't conclude the prayer. I praise God for my Bible-reading, prayer-believing Pentecostal mother.

After the KLM plane refueled, I saw it taxi by my window and disappear into the fog. A few minutes later our 747 slowly taxied down the same runway. The KLM jet was to taxi to the end of the runway and then around and takeoff on the same runway. We were to go part way down the runway and wait on a side ramp for our turn to takeoff.

Before we got to the ramp, our pilot saw the lights of the KLM in the distance. Of course, he thought these lights were stationary. And so he continued to taxi out on the runway, when suddenly, to his complete horror, he realized those lights were not stationary but, rather, were coming toward us at full takeoff speed of approximately 200 miles an hour. He tried desperately to get our 747 off the runway, but he didn't make it.

When the KLM came roaring out of the fog, the pilot decided the only thing to do was to attempt to take off over our plane. He got the nose of his plane over us, but the landing gear didn't make it, and came slicing through our jet, like a hot butcher knife going through butter. Our plane was cut in half, just a few rows in front of me in the tourist section. The front part of the plane fell forward and most of the people that survived were in that section. In our center section very few people lived, and in the tail section no one survived.

Immediately, upon impact, thousands of gallons of jet fuel came gushing through our section like a gigantic wave. Many people were saturated with the fuel and became flaming torches seconds later. I unfastened my seat belt and stood up, as explosions and fire engulfed the plane. To my left in the window seat was an 86-year-old woman, and next to her in the center seat was her 65-year-old daughter. Immediately in front of me, in the aisle seat, was my business partner. As I stood in the aisle, I looked to see if I could help the mother and daughter. It was too late. They were dead and on fire. I couldn't see Ted.

People were burning to death all around me. I could smell their hair burning and hear their screams. The cabin was a furnace, and the thick smoke made it difficult to see and breathe. Flying debris slashed into the flesh of the passengers and there was the sound of crushing grinding, exploding metal. It was hell on earth.

In the midst of this inferno, I could hear agonizing calls for help, mingled with loud cursing as people burned to death. It shocked me to hear cursing, because I thought if people were facing death, they would automatically call on God. From this experience, I now believe people die as they live. If in their life they have been blasphemers, they will blaspheme in the time of disaster and death.

I have been a Christian since 1932, and now, as the roaring flames seared those around me, portions of Scripture flashed through my mind: "I will never leave you or forsake you." "I am the god that will deliver you." "I am the same yesterday, and today, and forever." Then I began repeating Isaiah 43:1-2: "But now thus saith the Lord that created thee, O Jacob, and he that formed thee. . . . Fear not: for I have redeemed thee, I have called thee by thy name: thou art mine. When thou passest through the waters, I will be with thee; and through the rivers, they shall not overflow thee: when thou walkest through the fire, thou shalt not be burned; neither shall the flame kindle upon thee."

Then I began calling aloud to God: "I stand upon Your Word. I stand upon Your Word." As I was repeating these words, I saw a large chunk of debris hurtling toward me and I put both arms up, and with supernatural strength shoved it away. When I did this, I looked up for the first time since the crash and saw a large hole in the ceiling of the plane. The ceilings in 747's are at least ten feet high, but somehow I got through that hole. The metal was very jagged and razor sharp. My hands were shredded. It later took 40 stitches to save my fingers that were nearly slashed off.

It's a miracle how I was able to hurl my body over those sharp edges, because when you're 52 and weigh 260 pounds, you just don't do things like that anymore. But I got over without even ripping my clothes. Once I cleared the hole, I fell until I landed on the wing. It was difficult to keep my balance, because the wing was tilted and extremely slippery from jet fuel. The engines were still running, with fire raging in them. I knew the wing was full of fuel, and that it would be only a matter of seconds before the whole thing would go, because I could still hear explosions. I worked my way out on the wing and jumped to the ground. I'm told I fell about 30 feet. When I landed I shattered the bones in my left foot, but was able to hobble away from the plane. I heard two more explosions, and when I looked back our plane was gone.

I looked down the runway 150 yards and saw the KLM exploding violently. There were 250 passengers on that plane. No one survived![1]

What mysterious force picked up the 260 pound, 52-year-old Norman Williams and lifted him ten feet straight up through the top of the fuselage of the burning 747? Why, one of God's angels, no doubt!

Our good friend Rev. Hilton Sutton, gave us the following account of God's 24-hour emergency corps in action.

In a hurry to reach Memphis for a scheduled revival meeting, Hilton Sutton was traveling with a young evangelist friend and his wife on an icy highway in Iowa during the month of January. Suddenly, the car whirled into a vicious spin. Spinning on the ice-covered highway like a child's toy top, their automobile veered off the road and down a deep ditch to come eventually to rest against a solid embankment of rock and ice.

The three evangelists quickly scrambled out of the car and climbed out of the ditch to the edge of the highway. No sooner had they reached the highway than a huge wrecker pulled up to them.

Without saying a word, the driver jumped out, released the winch cable, hooked it onto the car, and pulled it back onto the highway. The wrecker driver then carefully turned the car so it was pointed in the right direction on the highway, unhooked the car, and rolled up the cable.

The driver then turned to the three evangelists standing in amazement watching with unbelieving eyes all that was taking place.

"I'll be seeing you," the driver said. And with those few words the driver was gone.

The wife of the young evangelist then cried out, "Look! Come quickly!"

They ran over to the car and looked in the back seat where she was pointing. The back seat had been lined with Christmas presents the young couple were carrying from home. To their amazement, not a box was out of place. Incredibly, nothing had fallen from the seat or from above the seat behind the window. They looked at the side of the car striking the embankment and discovered not the slightest scratch.

As they drove away, they looked for the wrecker. He left in such a rush they had not had time to offer payment or even thank him. To their astonishment the wrecker was nowhere in sight. There were no turnoff roads along the highway. The driver could not have left more than two or three minutes before they did, and could not have driven over 30 or 40 miles per hour on the icy road.

Rev. Hilton Sutton is sure God sent one of His angels to assist them in reaching their scheduled evangelistic meeting on time. It could have taken hours for help to have reached them along the deserted stretch of highway where the accident occurred.

[1] "Terror at Tenerife," reprinted from *VOICE* (April 1979), courtesy of the Full Gospel Business Men's Fellowship International, Costa Mesa, CA.

Chapter 20

Counseling with Angels

As my good friend Walt Field and I were praying together one evening in 1975, the Father spoke some startling words to us through prophecy.

The Lord said to us, "As you counsel together and consider what you shall do, be assured My angels are with you and shall sit in your meetings. They will always be with you as you plan how you shall prosper for the glory of God. My angels shall bring to you knowledge, ability, and wisdom. Wisdom and knowledge to solve difficult problems shall they impart to you as you consider what you shall do for the glory of the Lord. Yes, and the angels shall work for you and go before you and prosper your way in your ministry, your family, and your business."

This was a new revelation to us and we were completely surprised. Neither of us had ever thought of counseling with angels or considered the possibility of angels bringing knowledge and wisdom and answers to problems. We both prayed that evening and asked God to show us in His Word where an angel had ever been employed in such a way.

As I was sitting in church a few evenings later waiting for service to begin, I picked up my Bible and idly thumbed through it. I looked down to where my Bible lay open in my lap and the following Scriptures jumped up at me.

"Yes, while I was speaking in prayer, the man Gabriel, whom I had seen in the former vision, being caused to fly swiftly, came near to me and touched me about the time of the evening sacrifice. He instructed me and made me understand; he talked with me and said, O Daniel, I am now come forth to give you skill and wisdom and understanding" (Dan. 9:21-22;AMP).

I had read that Scripture before but had never realized that an angel brought wisdom and revelation knowledge to Daniel.

I also read in Daniel where God gave Daniel the ability to solve "knotty problems," as it says in the Amplified Bible. He was the administrator of the King's business.

Well, my friend Walt is a businessman, as well as an excellent Bible teacher and counselor. He has been in top management positions a number of years and has been instrumental in bringing about several dramatic turnarounds in sinking businesses. He is a leading authority on the practice of turning around management."

As well as a college professor and a writer, I am also a professional management consultant and enjoy working with Christian businessmen who are interested in earning finances for God's work.

Daniel was a management consultant, a trouble-shooter, a problem solver, and God raised him up to manage the Babylonian Empire. And his wisdom and knowledge came from an angel who counseled with him.

Then I knew that God had spoken through the prophecy. God was revealing to us that the same knowledge, wisdom, and ability to solve knotty problems Daniel displayed so brilliantly are available to Christian businessmen today who discipline themselves to follow God's instructions.

But, I yet lacked Scriptures in the New Testament, and I reminded the Father of our request. Then, in my spirit, I heard the Spirit say, "Don't you remember how an angel instructed Joseph to take the baby Jesus into Egypt because Herod sought to kill Him? And further, have you not read where the angel instructed Philip as to the direction he should take? And was not his ministry prospered as he obeyed? And then have you not read where Paul was counseled by an angel as to how to save a ship's crew? And, yet, again, have you considered how an angel appeared to Cornelius to direct him to salvation through Jesus Christ? And, did not all of these receive knowledge and wisdom from an angel?"

"Yes, Lord. Thank You, Father. Now I understand. Forgive my stupidity."

There could be no doubt. We have the covenant right to expect counsel from angels. But we will see the angels and be aware of their counsel only as God wills. We will accept the ministry of angels by faith like everything else we receive from God.

I am thoroughly convinced we are on the frontier of learning in this area. There are so many things in the Bible we have read over without discovering the meaning, either because our minds were not renewed or because of religious tradition.

If the first man, Adam, enjoyed such authority having angels as his servants and they obeyed his commands, what about the second Adam, God's own son? And what about that recreated born-again race known as New Testament believers? For He was the first-born of many and we are joint heirs. It is much too mind-boggling to conceive, so let's move on to something less startling.

If the angels work for us, would there be enough angels to go around? There are several references to the number of angels in the Bible (Heb. 12:22; Rev. 5:12). My friend Hilton Sutton told me just how many angels he has computed according to the Scriptures as we were having lunch together one day.

Hilton said, "There are one hundred trillion angels. Think about it like this. If there were four billion people living on planet Earth and one-half of them became believers, each Christian would have available to him 50,000 angels."

Fifty thousand angels for each man, woman, and child on the face of the earth! The way he jumped when he heard this, I thought our good friend J.C. Spencer was going to spill his coffee all over the table!

"If angels work 24 hours a day and never take coffee breaks or stop for lunch, just think what a work force a Christian businessman could have," J.C. Spencer said, quickly making a few calculations on his napkin. J.C. becomes excited over finding new ways to earn finances for the ministry.

Does God help Christian businessmen today? Will His angels work in our behalf to prosper our way, as the Scriptures say?

My long-time friend and Christian brother in Christ G.S. "Casey" Jones is convinced they do. When highly-educated engineers told him he couldn't move two barges, for they had tried and failed, Casey called on God for help. He couldn't explain to the barge owners how he was going to move them back to the water; he just knew in his spirit that God would show him how:

I guess our toughest job was when Hurricane Audrey washed two huge oil barges across Texas 87 near High Island and left the two valuable crafts stuck in the marsh. For $15,000 I promised to float those barges out into the gulf. If I failed, we would be paid nothing. These barges will float in just 24 inches of water, so I decided to build a dike around them and pump gulf water into the pond created by the dikes. The only problem was that there was a highly traveled state highway between the barges and the Gulf of Mexico and I'd promised the highway department the road wouldn't be damaged, left dirty, or closed at night. We closed it from daybreak to sunset — one day only.

We floated those barges up beside the road and then built another set of dikes on the gulf side of the highway. Then we built dikes across the highway with dump trucks, knocked down the dikes between the two lakes and floated those barges over the highway. We built a dike on the gulf side of the highway, let the water out of the first pond and re-opened the road. That afternoon around 4:30 the Lord sent a good ol' Beaumont hen-drowning, frog-strangling (that's Texas talk) rain and washed the highway as clean as a whistle.

We tried to build dikes out into the surf so we could float the barges out to sea, but the waves would knock down the dikes as fast as we built them. Then I tried Jesus! I just walked off down the beach and began to pray. "I'm stuck Lord," I said. "I've done all I know how to do. Show me the way to get these barges out of here." Then I repeated Jeremiah 33:3: "Call unto me, and I will answer thee, and show thee great and mighty things, which thou knowest not."

We'd been on the job for three weeks and I had a lot of money tied up in it. While thinking about this verse in Jeremiah a little ol' dog came around the toolhouse I'd set up for the job there. I pitched him a little piece of bread and he ate it and then started digging a hole in the sand. Then he looked up at me, just like he was making sure I was watching, and started to dig again. As he dug on the beach, water started filling up the hole. That dog had just shown me how to move those massive barges. I said, "Thanks, Lord, I got the message."

I told my operators to get the draglines and start digging till water seeped in at low tide. Well, we dug and dug and finally got that hole dug to the size of the barges. We filled the hole with water until the barges floated. We then broke the dikes on the gulf side. The water washed out in front, and at low tide we dug a channel to the barges. When the tide came in the barges floated free and a tug 1,500 feet offshore pulled them into the gulf. Our job was completed![2]

Who sent the rain and little dog and showed Casey how to move those barges? Very probably one of God's angels, just as the angel brought wisdom and knowledge to Daniel so that he could solve knotty problems.

[2] G.S. Jones, "We Move Anything," reprinted from *VOICE* (November 1978), courtesy of the Full Gospel Business Men's Fellowship International, Costa Mesa, CA.

Chapter 21

Angels as the Wind

"Who makes winds His messengers . . ." (Ps. 104:4).

"Referring to the angels, He says, 'He [God] makes His angels winds . . .' " (Heb. 1:7).

The above Scriptures present some very intriguing insight into the ministry of angels. Apparently, they may at times appear in the form of a wind, or the wind may serve as the announcement of a supernatural presence.

Just before David won a mighty battle against the Philistines, the Lord told him to wait until he heard a wind in the tops of the mulberry trees before going into battle. Very probably the sound in the trees was the movement of angels.

"And let it be, when thou hearest the sound of a going in the tops of the mulberry trees, that then thou shalt bestir thyself: for then shall the Lord go out before thee, to smite the host of the Philistines" (2 Sam. 5:24).

And, of course, on the day of Pentecost the presence of the Lord came as the sound of a mighty rushing wind. There are many present-day testimonies of church services where the power of God has moved through the auditorium like a rushing wind. This phenomenon is usually accompanied by miracles such as healings or many people experiencing the baptism of the Holy Spirit during the service.

Our friend Rev. Burnie Davis has given us some very exciting testimonies concerning his miraculous deliverances on the mission field when he asked God for supernatural wind. Burnie is convinced God does at times make His angels into winds of deliverance:

As David Slack, the pilot, circled the plane over the treetops, we could see

the villagers like scampering midgets running and waving their hands excitedly, while men in the plowed fields were leaving their oxen and running
through crooked rows at breakneck speed to get to their village for the exciting
event. In this remote region where a radio is a great treasure and a trip into a city is a
once-in-a-lifetime accomplishment, if at all, an airplane buzzing over the village is
one of life's big thrills.

"Okay, get ready, bombardier," David shouted above the roar of the wind from
the plane's open window.

David pulled the plane into an incredibly steep bank at precisely the right
moment, allowing for wind drift and altitude. One wing pointed upward toward God
and the other downward toward the creation of His hands and the object of His love.

"Now! Bombs away!" David screamed.

For a split second I looked straight down through the open window at the
brown-skinned people below.

"Father, in the Name of Jesus, anoint your Word to their hearts," I prayed. And
then I let the bombs slide through my hands downward to the extended arms and
hungry hearts of the excited villagers.

Our bombs were copies of the Gospel of John and announcements of our
forthcoming crusade in a nearby city. As the booklets tumbled crazily through the
air, tossed by the prop wash, the villagers scattered like ants on an anthill, trying
desperately to catch the precious Gospels before they hit the ground.

David quickly pulled the red and white Cherokee back so that the wings were
level, then opened the throttle and raised the flaps. Through the still-open window I
could see the people and houses become smaller and then lost in the distance as the
plane burrowed into a thick mountain of fluffy white clouds.

"Via con Dios, God go with you," I said.

"Amen," Ruben said from the back seat.

David climbed to 2,500 feet, then leveled the plane off as we headed down river
for the next village.

It was customary on each planned bombing mission to drop Gospels in as many villages as our supply would allow. We bombed six additional villages along the river, and then headed home to our hotel room in Veracruz to pray and otherwise prepare for our large crusade in the ball parks the next day.

Bombing missions completed for the day, we began noticing the breathtaking beauty of the great river below us. The water was peaceful and calm and the jungle seemed to fold over into the river along the banks. Huge lily pads with bright red and white flowers floated on the crystal clear water.

"Let's go down a little closer and take a look," Dave suggested.

It was against my better judgment, but I could not resist the temptation to survey this wondrous beauty of God's handiwork anymore than could Dave. So down Dave went to within 50 or 60 feet of the great body of water. At this close range we could see the fish jumping in the water.

"Quick, Dave hand me your camera," I said.

I pointed the camera toward the river and pushed the button, but nothing happened.

"Hey, Dave, how do you take a picture with this thing anyway?" I asked in disgust at having missed a beautiful scene. Dave quickly showed me how to turn the film to another picture and we both looked up at the same time.

"Oh, my God help us," David screamed.

Across the river directly in front of us stretched three federal power lines as large as my index finger. It was too late! We were right upon the lines and could not go either over or under them.

David flew right into the ominous high voltage lines which were supported on either bank by gigantic steel towers.

"Oh, God, we need a miracle," I prayed as the wires popped against the plane. The windshield shattered, and sparks flew everywhere. We seemed suspended in air with no motion for a split second, and then the plane headed down and toward the dense jungle on the left bank of the river.

I have heard that your life passes before you in a brief second when you face certain death. But I was too busy praying and trying to figure out how to stay alive.

"Dave, don't land in the trees, man! Set her down in the water! We'll have a chance in the river!" I screamed out in a split second in one breath.

Then Ruben spoke up from the back seat in his slow English drawl. "Brother, is the wing supposed to be like that?"

David and I both popped our heads toward the wing where Ruben pointed. The aileron had been knocked loose on the left wing and stood straight up from the wing seven or eight feet. That's the reason the plane was flying to the left so suddenly.

"Oh, God help us," David prayed. "We've got to get this plane on the ground."

"Set it down in the river," I repeated again. Neither one of us knew what to do.

David tried to turn the plane away from the left bank of the river just before we hit the trees. Miraculously, the left wing lifted and David headed back over the river.

"Thank You, Jesus, for a miracle," we all three prayed.

David said, "Burnie, I've got to set it down in the river."

"You're still flying, David. Look for an open field," I screamed out in a high, shrill voice.

After a minute or two the plane was still flying over the river without dipping back to the left bank.

"I am going to check it out and see what kind of control we have," David said.

"Man, whatever you do, be careful," I said looking toward the thick jungle on either side of the river and all of a sudden wondering how big the alligators grew in the river.

David eased the plane to a higher altitude and found he had perfect control when he turned in either direction.

We all three began shouting and praising God for a mighty miracle. David flew on to a small airport some 15 minutes away. When we approached the airport, we decided not to change air speed as we knew the plane would fly at the present speed. So we landed with flaps up in excess of 100 miles per hour.

"Thank You, Jesus, for another miracle!"

On the ground again, we inspected the plane. The prop was badly damaged, the aileron was completely torn from the wing on one end. Everywhere there were cuts and gashes in the wings, tail, and body. The gas cap was even missing. It was aerodynamically impossible for the plane to fly in that condition.

But, praise God, the angels came as the wind and bore up the wings of that little red and white plane. God is still in the business of performing miracles for His children.[1]

Another very dramatic example of God's angels ministering as the wind occurred during the Israeli Six Day War. General Rabin, who later became prime minister of Israel, was to lead his troops through the Sinai on one of the most strategic missions of the war.

When they reached the Sinai, to their dismay they discovered the area had been mined for miles. There was no way around. They had to go through the mines at the risk of their lives, because the continued existence of their nation depended on these soldiers.

Bravely, the soldiers entered the mined area without hesitation, knowing for many it would be a death march. Just as the first of the advance troops entered the mined fields, a tremendous wind began blowing desert dust in gigantic swirls. The great wind blew quickly throughout the several miles of the mined area. Then, just as suddenly as it had started, it died down. The desert was again quiet.

The Israeli troops watching in amazement. Before them lay the exposed tops of the Egyptian mines for as far as they could see. It was an easy matter to simply maneuver around the exposed mines and quickly reach their destination to the surprise of the enemy.

The Yahweh of Israel, the God of Abraham, Isaac, and Jacob, had remembered the everlasting covenant He had made with Israel. Michael and his angels had come to fight for Israel.

Chapter 22

Angels on the Mission Field

The apostles of the New Testament were often rescued, protected, or otherwise ministered to by angels. The word *apostle* actually means "sent ones," and the modern-day missionary is the counterpart of the early day apostle.

Of course, we are all familiar with the stories of angelic deliverances of the apostles as recorded in the New Testament. For instance, we read in Acts 12 of the angel delivering Peter from prison. And, in Acts 27 is recorded the account of Paul talking with an angel as he stood on the heaving deck of a sinking ship.

But, is it still happening today, we might wonder. Are angels still ministering on the front lines of evangelism as modern-day apostles or missionaries carry the Gospel to dark lands? The answer is a thundering YES! In this chapter are a few testimonials, fresh from the mission field.

Rev. A.N. Trotter spent 12 years in Africa as a missionary. While preaching in a camp meeting, he related this fascinating story. Trotter pastored a church in Cape Palmas, Liberia, West Africa. One Sunday morning while in service, the front door of the church suddenly burst open. A very excited young man rushed in shouting in his native tongue.

At first, the congregation thought he was demon-possessed. But the Spirit of God revealed to Trotter that this was not the case. After the young man had finally calmed down, someone in the church was able to understand his dialect.

He was from the Belera tribe and had traveled several hundred miles to Cape Palmas. His tribe had never heard of Jesus Christ and had never been visited by a missionary. But in his heart he knew there had to be a great spirit being. To his amazement, an angel appeared and told him to go to Cape Palmas where he would find a preacher who would tell him about God.

Some may wonder why the angel did not tell him about Jesus Christ. Only man is given the distinct privilege of proclaiming the gospel message.

Then the young man told how he had entered Cape Palmas and saw a big church. He started to open the door when the angel appeared again and told him not to go in because he would not find God there. He continued running and came upon another church, and the same scene was repeated.

Finally, he ran one more and this time found the church that Brother Trotter pastored. The angel appeared again and told him this was the right one. He had finally found the place where he could find God.

Angels also protect modern day missionaries, acting as private bodyguards as they once did for the New Testament apostles. Rev. Bill Loveck, missionary to Africa for years, gave the following fascinating testimonial while ministering at Victory Assembly of God Church in Beaumont, Texas.

Bill Loveck felt impressed of the Lord to begin ministering to a tribe of cannibals who had never been visited by a white man. When he related this message to his African Bible school student and guide, the young man became very upset. That particular tribe was also notorious for eating the flesh of the young man's tribe.

Finally, Loveck persuaded the young man that God was with them and would send His angels to protect them. They traveled by jeep for several days into the African bush. Occasionally at night they heard the roar of a full-grown lion as they slept in the open jeep. The young African stirred uneasily, but Loveck assured him God's angels would protect them.

Once, just before reaching the village of their destination, they heard many voices and the rustling of bushes during the night. The next morning they discovered a circle of spears and knives around their jeep, as if would-be attackers had left in a hurry.

After reaching the village the next day and telling the simple gospel message of Jesus Christ, they witnessed the salvation of nearly the whole tribe, including the chief. Also saved were the group of young warriors who had attacked the jeep the night before. Immediately after accepting Christ, they excitedly inquired as to the whereabouts of the two giant men with glowing white robes and long gleaming swords who stood on either side of the jeep each night. The two men in white apparel had suddenly appeared when the warriors approached the jeep. Frightened almost out of their wits, they dropped the weapons and ran from the supernatural beings.

Rev. H.B. Garlock was for many years a missionary to Africa. In his best-selling book *Before We Kill and Eat You*, he tells how God sent His angels to deliver them from the hand of a cannibalistic tribe:

After the service was over the chief instructed his head wife to prepare a tasty meal for his guest, the white man. Shortly, she appeared with a calabash of cooked rice and an earthen bowl of soup cooked with palm nuts. The woman tasted the rice and soup in our presence to prove that the food had not been poisoned. The carrion rat meat made it taste like poison to us, but the abundance of red pepper used in its preparation helped to cover a "multitude of sins." It was said that if the guest of a chief in that tribe refused to eat the food set before him, the woman who prepared it would be killed as a witch. Therefore, to save the poor woman's life, we prayed. "Dear Lord, sanctify the food and please don't let it kill us." It didn't!

It was customary for our carriers, when on trek, to spend the night scattered about in various huts throughout the village. But that night all of them were very eager to stay in the same hut with me. After committing ourselves to God's watchful care, we turned in for the night.

About midnight I was suddenly awakened by the sound of tom-toms and blood-curdling screams. I immediately rose from my cot and looked through the only opening in the hut, a small doorway facing in the direction from which we had come earlier in the evening. To my consternation I saw a mass of black humanity pouring through the north gate of the village, screaming and yelling at the top of their voices. Each one carried a weapon, and I heard them shouting, "Where is the white man? We have come to kill the white man! We know he is in this town, and if you don't tell us where he is, we'll burn your town to the ground!"

I saw one of the frightened townspeople point to the hut where we were staying. That was all the signal they needed; they made a mad rush in our direction. their wild cries awakened John Yeddah and the rest of our party. I can almost see dear old John yet, as he came over to the opening and knelt beside me. "Look at them!" he said. "Did you ever see such wild people? Do you hear what they are saying?"

"Yes," I assured him, "I hear altogether too well." As we watched they halted in the middle of the open space before us, where there were several human skulls, an elephant skull, and a huge rock which was used by the people of the village for a whetstone for sharpening their hunting and farm implements. We saw these men sharpen their weapons and take an oath, the strongest oath in the tribe, which oath included drinking their own urine from the hand, that they would neither eat nor sleep until they had killed and feasted upon the white man.

John turned to me with tears in his eyes, saying, "Mr. Garlock, what shall we do?" I replied that there was only one thing we could do, and that was to PRAY. And pray we did. Our little group poured out their hearts to God in earnest supplication. We certainly did not search for flowery words, but cried out to God to have mercy upon us and help us. That little hut became the gateway to heaven that night. I remember asking the Lord to forgive me where I had blundered and done the wrong thing, to overlook my ignorance and help us out of our predicament. I reminded the Lord that we had come, we believed, in His will in answer to a dying woman's prayer, and that my wife and the other Christians were praying for the success of our trip and would never know what happened to us if we fell into the hands of this bloodthirsty mob.

Then the Scripture in Psalm 34:7 came to me: "The angel of the Lord encampeth round about them that fear him, and delivereth them." While in prayer I felt impressed to go outside the hut and face the angry mob. I told John how I felt. He begged me to stay inside, and offered to go himself and try to appease the infuriated mob. He said if they killed him it didn't matter, but I must not go. This brave man meant it with all his heart. I told John, "It is I they want, not you. You just continue to hold onto God in prayer."

I stepped out into the opening. Jitueh and all my porters stayed hidden inside the hut, frightened almost to death. John came to the doorway to try to help me with the language. It was a beautiful moonlit night and I was quickly observed. The mob rushed forward and soon surrounded the hut. I tried to talk and reason with them, but it was useless. They had been drinking palm wine and had worked themselves into an angry frenzy.

As was the custom, these men had each of their front teeth filed to a sharp point, and their hair braided into long, woolly pigtails. Their faces were painted with war paint and their quivering bodies were greased with palm oil. Their long knives and cutlasses gleamed in the moonlight. When I saw they were too wild to listen to reason, I said, as calmly as I could, "You have taken your vows and made your threats, but I am trusting in my God to protect me."

They made a mad rush toward me with drawn knives, shouting, "Kill him, kill!" The leader rushed at me with his cutlass raised to behead me. When it seemed the end had come and my head was about to be severed from my body, I closed my eyes and committed myself to God, repeating over and over that one name that is above every name, "JESUS, JESUS!"

Suddenly there was a death-like stillness! The tom-toms stopped beating and all screaming and yelling halted abruptly. The silence could almost be felt. After what seemed like hours I cautiously opened my eyes, and wondered if I could believe them! Before me stood some of the savages with their weapons upraised ready to strike, while others held drawn knives by their sides. But all were frozen in their tracks, including my would-be executioner. The God who closed the lions' mouths in Daniel's time had held these wild, angry cannibals at bay! God had done what reasoning and persuasion could not do.

Too spellbound to move, I waited breathlessly to see what would happen next. Presently they began to relax, slowly backing up, and withdrew to the center of the village around the great rock where they held a hurried consultation. After some discussion the leader came toward me, bowing to the ground at intervals as he came. I was still standing in front of the hut as though in a dream. This man seized me by the ankles and began to plead with me to have mercy on him and his men and spare their lives. "We see that the white man's God fights for him," he said. "If you will forgive us we will accept your terms for settling the palaver."

I told them we wished them no harm. Since they were ready to come to terms we would be glad to pay them the price of little Jitueh's redemption so that she might be free to return to her dying mother. They readily agreed, so we measured out to them several yards of blue trading cloth, a supply of salt, and other commodities amounting to the price of a full-grown Pahn woman. In addition to this, I gave them a blanket for their chief and some trinkets for the young men who would be carrying the loads back to the village.

After accepting the goods, for which they thanked me, an order was given by their leader. They resumed the beating of the tom-toms and with a mad rush disappeared into the African night.

It was not until the noise of yelling and drumming had died away in the distance that I fully realized what had happened. I still do not know what they saw that night, but I have often wondered if they saw an angel of the Lord, as mentioned in Psalm 34:7. Or, perhaps, like Elisha's servant of old, they saw the horses and chariots of fire encircling our little company. One thing is certain they did feel and see something that caused them to know that God was there protecting His servants. God had performed a miracle before our very eyes.[1]

[1] H.B. Garlock, *Before We Kill and Eat You* (Dallas, TX: Christ For The Nations, 1974), p. 86-90. Used by permission.

Chapter 23

Angels Over the Nations

Everyone agrees that the moral fabric of our society is unraveling. It seems to be coming about through some sort of design. Who or what is so desperately trying to destroy our great nation?

The apostle Paul wrote the answer many years ago. In this chapter, we will attempt to expound upon Paul's succinct explanation. Paul said in Ephesians 6:12-18, "For we wrestle not against flesh and blood, but against principalities, against powers, against the rulers of the darkness of this world, against spiritual wickedness in high places. Wherefore take unto you the whole armor of God, that ye may be able to withstand in the evil day, and having done all, to stand. Stand therefore, having your loins girt about your feet shod with the preparation of the gospel of peace; above all, taking the shield of faith, wherewith ye shall be able to quench all the fiery darts of the wicked. And take the helmet of salvation, and the sword of the Spirit, which is the word of God; Praying always with all prayer and supplication in the spirit, and watching thereunto with all prayer and supplication in the Spirit, and watching there unto with all perseverance and supplication for all saints."

Daniel had an unusual experience in which the angel Gabriel was detained while bringing a message concerning the nation Israel. Gabriel was held in captivity by a spirit being reported to be the prince of Persia, an enemy to Israel. The angel Michael, who called himself the Prince of Israel, came to the assistance of Gabriel and quickly overpowered the prince of Persia, sending Gabriel on his way with the important message.

In this brief passage of Scripture, several interesting facts concerning angels and other spirit beings are revealed.

First, it is important to note that spirit beings identify themselves with nations that are actually in existence. Not fictional nations or spiritually and religiously categorized nations, but nations that can be identified on a map.

Second, there is a real power struggle in the spirit world for control of these nations. The spirit world conflict can be identified very readily in the natural world by looking at the conflict among existing nations. In Daniel's time it was the nation of Israel, God's chosen people, against the nations aligned with the world system including Persia. Today, it is the free world against the nations with oppresive governments. The same basic conflicts are still in existence.

The third interesting fact derived from this Scripture is the types of angels involved. Apparently, the angel Gabriel is primarily a messenger angel and does not possess the warrior ability of the fearsome Michael. This concurs with present day believers' experiences with angels as reported in the chapter entitled "Worshiping with Angels." Here, it was found that two basic types of angels made appearances to believers — warrior angels and messenger angels.

Now we begin to understand why there is so much trouble across the world. The explanation is Satan's attack on nations still standing for basic beliefs in Christ. These nations must be done away with before he can set up his kingdom. *But Satan must work through men. He must find men who will yield themselves to him.* Satan is limited in this way just as God has limited himself.

To learn what Satan is doing, simply look at the nations whose leaders have yielded themselves to Satan. The result of his leadership is easy to see — wars, destruction, wanton killings, millions of Jews put to torture and horrible deaths by a crazed, demon-possessed maniac who almost gained control of the world except for God's intervention, as we shall learn in a later chapter.

But why does Satan so desperately desire full control of the world? Actually, the great ambition of Satan remains unchanged from the beginning since his fall from heaven and rule with God. Satan wants to be God. He wants to be worshiped. He is full of pride, selfishness, and self-seeking.

Satan's activity today is multifarious and diabolical. He is limited in his powers, though his influence in the earth is pervasive. Since subtly and nefariously deceiving and defeating our first parents, he has continuously sought complete control of the world. Satan is identified in the Scriptures as the prince of this world, the god of this world, and the prince of the power of the air (John 14:30; 2 Cor. 4:4; Eph. 2:2).

Satan's great tool, as at the beginning, is deception. He is a liar and the father of lies according to John 8:44. Satan never fights fairly, but always uses subterfuge, beguilement, and delusion. He most often seeks to hide his real identity.

Satan's desire is that men believe he does not exist, that all mention of him is mystical, or that he is actually a jolly fellow meaning no ill harm at all. Satan deceives the rulers of nations in a slightly different way. He offers power, real power to rule and control the world, to certain men who will worship him.

Remember that he offered Jesus the kingdoms of the earth if Jesus would fall down and worship him. Apparently Satan possessed the power and authority to offer rule of the world, because Jesus did not deny that he had such power in his rebuttal.

Many Christians expect to see Satan's work only among the filthy dregs of society. It is easy to see Satan's work among criminals, prostitutes, drug addicts, and alcoholics. But, seemingly, it has always been difficult for the Christian to recognize the work of Satan in influential circles, the super rich, and government leaders. But the truth is, he would much prefer to work in the influential circles of the earth.

Satan went to the top when he offered control of the world system to Jesus, did he not? Can it be assumed that he does not offer world control to influential world leaders today? The truth is, he is doing and has done just that. And, unlike Jesus, who defeated Satan's deceptive offer, men in our time have accepted Satan and are using his power and cunning ability to gain complete and absolute control of the world. This must come to pass to pave the way for the coming of the Antichrist world system, or the rule of Satan.

During Satan's soon-coming rule, millions who refuse to worship him as god will be put to a torturous death. It will be the greatest blood bath in the history of the world. It is urgent that Christians do all they can now to reach the world for Christ.

So why is Satan so desperate to destroy America? We are the nation primarily responsible for ministering the gospel around the world. We are a nation whose God is the Lord and whose Saviour is Jesus Christ, the living Son of God. Satan's blood boils when he thinks about it. If he could destroy this great nation, he could take the world.

So, what is he doing to take this nation, and what can the Christian do about it? First, if we Christians rise up and obey God, Satan will not be able to destroy our nation until God is through using it to spread the gospel message around the world. The Bible firmly states the church of Jesus Christ shall be built or established and the gates, or leaders, of hell shall not prevail, or hold out, against it (Matt. 16:18).

The Christian is victorious and should not act in fear. To act in fear is what Satan and his human leaders want us to do. No, Satan cannot take this nation unless the Christians sit back and allow him to do it. Unless we give it to him, he won't have it. When God is through with our nation and the Christians are taken out, then Satan can have the United States and rot with it.

Why is our great nation so terribly in debt? Why do we rely on oil supplies from thinly-veiled enemies? Why the taxes which make it so increasingly difficult to survive from one paycheck to the next? (Note: This chapter was published in 1979.)

The answer is that all of the above have been carefully planned, designed, and engineered by a handful of the world's super rich families who desire one-world government so they may rule the world.

Stranglehold control of the finances of this nation was gained in the early 1900s. Their influence and control is felt by many major corporations in our nation, and especially the oil industry, for control of the world's energy supply was one of their major goals. The key word is CONTROL, not necessarily outright ownership. Control is less conspicuous and more convenient than outright ownership.

True to Satan's subtle form, the doctrine of humanism rather than outright Marxist philosophies is promulgated in our nation. The God-hating and Goddenouncing doctrine of other world governments would be easily rejected in our nation. But the even more deadly doctrine of humanism is more subtle, more deceptive, and easier to get across without detection.

Christians continue to sleep, while demons from hell operating through the minds of men, rape our school system, taking out the mention of the name of God and any type of prayer and substituting witchcraft and the doctrine of humanism.

The Americans have been taken to the cleaners and it is our own fault. We are in the position Daniel was in when he prayed for his nation Israel to be delivered from Babylonian captivity. God heard Daniel's prayer and sent an angel to answer.

Will God hear the prayers of Americans today? A thundering, "Yes," God shouts down from heaven. Paul admonished us to pray for the leaders of our government in 1 Timothy 2:1-2. This we must do every day. In addition, Daniel called for the aid of angels for his nation. This we also do as plainly shown in the chapter entitled "Our New Covenant Right to Use Angels."

The Christian's right is to ask God to send ministering angels to strengthen, advise, and counsel with the leaders of our nation. Daniel was a statesman and a leader of Israel. The angel brought wisdom and knowledge to Daniel.

The Christian needs to know that those who seek to control our great nation are sending demon spirits to influence the decisions of our government leaders. But just as Michael overpowered the prince of Persia, so can God's angels overcome the influence of demonic spirits on our nation's leaders. Yes, the angels can and will form a protective hedge about our national leaders so the demon spirits cannot influence decisions made in our government.

Christian, think about it! Think it through and then act on the new information you have just been given. If you doubt the truth of what you have just read, if you doubt that our great nation is in jeopardy of control of the proponents of New World Order with the intent of world control, then take the time to investigate for yourself. Keep an open mind. Read your Bible daily and you will discover what is going on in the world today as the path is prepared for the rise and rule of Satan incarnated in the flesh, the biblical Antichrist, through the coming New World Order.

In Revelation 13:3-4 we discover the world will become Satan worshipers under the reign of the Antichrist. "And I saw one of his heads as it were wounded to death; and his deadly wound was healed: and all the world wondered after the beast. And they worshipped the dragon which gave power unto the beast: and they worshiped the beast saying, Who is like unto the beast? Who is able to make war with him?"

The proponents of New World Order have spent years and billions of dollars contriving and manipulating to control the world's oil and coal reserves and the world's refineries. It reminds one of the great effort Satan put himself through to put Jesus Christ on the Cross, only to find he had played right into the hands of God. Satan committed the second most devastating mistake of his life when he put sinless Christ on the Cross. The first mistake was when he revolted against God.

When we look behind the scenes at what is going on in our world, we discover the spirit world is highly organized. The real decisions and the real battles are fought and either won or lost in the spirit world. Actually, the natural world is simply a mirror image of events occurring in the spirit world.

Bless the Lord, O you his angels, you mighty ones who do his word, hearkening to the voice of his word! (Ps. 103:20;RSV).

As a point of reference and standard for exploring the purposes and pursuits of angels, a biblical world view has been presented throughout this book. However, one who is not a proponent of a Christian Bible would necessarily have to admit to the existence of a spiritual world in order to even accept the existence of spiritual beings such as angels. This, then, requires the adherence to a spiritualistic world view, not necessarily Christian, which is adhered to by far a majority of the earth's nearly six billion inhabitants.

Every civilized society throughout history has always upheld some form of moral law such as the Ten Commandments of the Bible. Actually, throughout the western world, the Ten Commandments have been an integral part of the law of the land. For example, all of the original colonies in early America adapted their laws from the law of the Bible. In fact, in the famous Leyden Agreement, the pilgrims stress that they would obey all the laws of King James of England in the new land so long as no law ever conflicted with the Holy Scriptures.

This idea of American national law coincided with biblical law which carried over to the U.S. Supreme Court where it became known as the Natural Law. The common interpretation of the Natural Law meant that all United States law must meet two major criteria: no law would conflict with the laws of nature and no law would conflict with the law of the Bible. Judge Clarence Thomas referred often to the Natural Law when facing the nominating committee of the U.S. Senate during his confirmation to the U.S. Supreme Court.

Why is this so important to our understanding of the workings of angels among the nations? Clearly the Scriptures teach that the angels work in behalf of those who keep the covenant, and the heart of the covenant of the Bible is the Ten Commandments. In fact, the Bible is the book containing all spiritual law.

It would seem to logically follow then, if we use the principles of spiritual law as found in the Bible as our standard point of reference, that the angels would work in behalf of those nations whose national laws correspond with the Ten Commandments and the spiritual law of the Bible. This idea could be proven by studying the example of biblical Israel. Whenever Israel kept the covenants of spiritual law, the heart of which was the Ten Commandants, Israel prospered greatly and was most blessed among nations. However, Israel always ran into severe national problems whenever their national law conflicted with their original covenants.

It is interesting to note that England came out of national illiteracy during the 1500s by learning to read the Bible. Historians saw this expanding vocabulary of English during the 1500s as parallel to England's emergence as a world power. It was said that "the sun never set on the British Empire." But when the covenants of the spiritual law were all but forgotten, England began to decline as a world power.

America is a nation which seems to closely parallel biblical Israel in rise to prominence as the covenants of spiritual law were closely maintained.

America became the single greatest nation that the world has ever known. However, similar also to biblical Israel, America has begun a steady decline since national laws have been in conflict with the basic covenants of spiritual law.

The welfare of a nation would seem to depend, at least in part, on the activity of angels reacting to that nation's obedience to the covenants of spiritual law. America and biblical Israel are prime examples which seem to prove that angels work to the benefit of nations which keep the basic covenants of spiritual law. The following show this to certainly be a principle of the Bible.

> The angel of the Lord encamps around those who fear Him [who revere and worship Him with awe] and each of them He delivers (Ps. 34:7).

> To such as keep His covenant [hearing, receiving, loving, and obeying it] and to those who earnestly remember His commandments to do them [imprinting them on their hearts]. The Lord has established His throne in the heavens, and His kingdom rules over all. Bless (affectionately, great fully praise) the Lord you His angels, you mighty ones who do His commandments, harkening the voice of His Word (Ps. 103:18-20;AMP).

What might we expect in America as the nations of the world move more closely to the New World Order? If we continue to follow the example of biblical Israel in predicting what will happen in America as America continues to violate spiritual law, we can see that America will as a nation, face more severely difficult problems such as more violent crime, deeper debt, high interest rates, inflation, higher prices for food and oil, further moral decay, and increases in physical and mental illness. All of the above will continue to plague America as America heads down the road to becoming a Third World nation.

Oil will again increase in price as trouble breaks out in the Middle East.

this will cause a return of inflation. As the government removes price supports for farm commodities, all but the larger grain farms will be forced to quit growing grains. This, coupled with severe weather, will cause an eventful dramatic increase in grain prices worldwide, and sometime in the future will lead to the rationing of foodstuffs.

The stock market will climb higher, with corrections of course, until the final plug is pulled and it comes tumbling down. Great fortunes will be lost overnight. This will be like the shot heard around the world as the economies of nations fall like dominoes. Jobs will be lost and crime will run rampant in the streets. This will lead to international marshal law and America will become a virtual police state for a while. This will continue until the American people are fed up with crime and economic problems and are ready to surrender America's sovereignty for the peace, prosperity, and security promised by the proponents of the New World Order.

But it doesn't have to end this way. America can once again become a blessed nation:

> If my people, which are called by my name, will humble themselves, and pray, and seek my face, and turn from their wicked ways, then will I hear from heaven, forgive their sin, and heal their land (Chron. 7:14).

But whether America repents and is healed or not, one thing is certain. There will be a great spiritual awakening move across the whole earth. The recent increased interest in angels is evidence of its beginning.

One who doubts the workings of angels among the nations should consider the ancient city of Jerusalem. All of the mighty kingdoms that once surrounded Jerusalem have been eclipsed. Of all the cities founded by the ancients, Jerusalem alone retains their ancient glory and a special destiny with God.

Chapter 24

Angels in the Israeli Six-Day War

If the nation Israel faced a time of great peril during World War II, and certainly they did, it was nothing to compare with the many threats against their survival as a nation since 1948. We have received firsthand accounts of the holocaust in which six million Jews lost their lives from surviving brothers, sisters, sons, and daughters of those who were so brutally tortured to death. This was a terrible time for the Jews. But becoming a nation did not end the problems.

God told Daniel that His commander, Michael, was on a special assignment to see that the nation Israel survived during the most perilous period of their existence (Dan. 12:1-2). Surely, when the vast armies of Egypt moved against this tiny nation of less than two million in 1967, Israel faced one of the greatest threats for survival since becoming a nation in 1948.

Our good friend Rev. Hilton Sutton, who has a tremendously successful ministry to the Israelis, related to us the following accounts of angels fighting for Israel in the Six-Day War. Sutton received the stories directly from Israeli General Mordecai Gur as he sat across the banquet table from Israel's national hero and most distinguished general just five weeks after the Six-Day War.

During the first 30 minutes of the Six-Day War, Israel moved with such surprise that the military back of all the Arab nations was completely broken. The other five days, 23 hours and 30 minutes of the war were but mopping-up exercises.

In a previous story we related the story of General Rabin's move through the Sinai, an area heavily mined, to stage a surprise attack against the enemy. A great wind came up and blew across the desert, exposing the top of every mine.

Later, in that same area of the Sinai, 5,000 Egyptian troops with over 200 pieces of artillery and tanks surrendered to less than 100 Israeli soldiers with 2 tanks. Incredible? It couldn't happen, you say?

The Israeli general who related these accounts of the war is not religious.

How did it happen? When the Egyptian officers were interrogated separately by the Israelis, the following report was given by each officer. Each Egyptian officer said he saw Israeli troops advancing against them by the thousands, and each heard the roar of many hundreds of Israeli tanks.

The Egyptian officers said they knew they were outnumbered and outgunned. To save the lives of their troops they just threw up their hands and surrendered.

What happened? The answer is obvious. Michael, Chief of Staff of the Armies of Heaven, was there on assignment. Suddenly, he caught sight of 100 Israeli troops in serious trouble in the desert. Michael sent angelic reinforcements to aid the Israelis. Those Egyptian officers were convinced they saw thousands of soldiers and heard hundreds of tanks. And they were right. What they saw and heard were part of the armies of heaven under Michael's command.

In the Old Testament, God said Israel's enemies would come against them one way and flee in seven ways. One soldier would put 10 to flight and 2 soldiers could defeat 100 of the enemy. It is just as true today as it was then.

The Jordanians were late getting involved in the Six-Day War. But when they did get into the war, they had the best vantage point of anybody. Jordan held the west bank of the Jordan River and they still held the old biblical city of Jerusalem. The only thing separating the old city of Jerusalem from the new city of Jerusalem was a barbed wire fence, an entanglement of wire.

And across that barbed wire entanglement was the Jordanian artillery, the very best American and British field pieces available. All were pointed at Israel at point-blank range. All were manned by well-trained artillerymen.

The hour came for the Jordanians to enter the war. The command came to open fire on Israel, across the street in the new city of Jerusalem. The expert artillerymen fired their new field pieces at strategic targets, all at point-blank range.

Surely this was Israel's Waterloo. The city of Jerusalem could not possibly survive. Could not survive, except for divine intervention by Michael and his army.

Michael was aware of what was about to happen. The Jordanian artillerymen opened fire on the nation of Israel, just across the street. What happened?

When the Jordanians fired those big 105s, they missed the whole nation of Israel. Those 105s landed in the Mediterranean Sea with a big splash. Try as they may, the Jordanian expert artillerymen could not hit Israel across the street.

What happened? Michael sent an angel to each artillery piece, and every time the Jordanians fired, the angel just reached up and gave it a tap and changed the trajectory. The angels just thumped the 105s right into the sea.

There are many other accounts of divine intervention in which confusion was sent to the Arabs and they knocked out their own tanks and heavy armor with their own air force or with their own artillery. In these instances, the pilots or soldiers heard the wrong coordinates on their radios and knocked out their own equipment. Very similar to what happened in the bible when God sent a spirit of confusion among the enemies of Israel so that thousands fled from Gideon's 300 men with candlesticks as their only weapon.

When flying on a Swiss jet to Israel some months after the war, I asked the stewardess how she thought the Israelis won the war against such great odds. Without hesitation, she replied, "Why, God fights for the Israelis, of course."

It was late evening when the giant aircraft approached Tel Aviv. Below me were the thousands of lights of a very prosperous and successful nation. I thought, *Yes, God does fight for the Israelis.*

But God also fights for the Christian. And His angels are with us to preserve and protect us just as much as they are with Israel.

As the wheels of the jet touched down on Israeli soil, a great surge of faith flowed through my spirit. The same God and His angels who enabled Israel to win a war against such astronomical odds was also my God, and His angels were with me 24 hours a day.

Chapter 25

Michael, Chief of Staff of the Armies of Heaven

The angel Michael is associated with war and fighting throughout the Scriptures. In Revelation 12, John says that Michael and his angels will make war against Satan and overcome Satan and all his angels. The wording here indicates convincingly that Michael is in charge of the armies of heaven. Only to Michael is the term archangel or high angel specifically applied in the Scriptures.

Also, Michael has a special assignment to fight for and protect Israel. For in Daniel 12:1-2 we read, "And at that time shall Michael stand up, the great prince which standeth for the children of the people: and there shall be a time of trouble, such as never was since there was a nation even to that same time: and at that time thy people shall be delivered, every one that shall be found written in the book."

Here God tells Daniel that the great archangel Michael, the mighty warrior, shall have the special assignment to preserve Israel. Though the nation will go through devastating circumstances, the nation will survive, all 12 tribes of Israel. All that have their name written in the book. And all 12 tribes are in the Bible.

Now Satan would take great delight in destroying the nation Israel. First, Israel is God's own special people, the race in covenant relationship with God. Second, if Israel could be destroyed, then God's Word would be made null and void. God would be put in the position of having broken His prophetic Word. Satan would win a tremendous victory against God if he could cause the great Creator of the universe to break His own Word.

Thus, we see why Satan is so intent on destroying the nation Israel. Many times in the past the angels have fought for Israel. The Old Testament is full of stories of angelic intervention on behalf of Israel.

For example, King Hezekiah received a threatening letter from the Assyrian army general. Hezekiah took the letter immediately into the house of the Lord and spread it out for God to read (2 Kings 19:14-19).

"Look, God, what they are saying about You," Hezekiah said.

Hezekiah didn't say, "Look, Lord at what the Assyrians are saying about Israel." No, he said look at what they said about God. For Hezekiah was well aware of his covenant rights with God. When an enemy attacked Israel, it was as though God himself were being attacked. For Israel and God had become one under the Abrahamic blood covenant.

So that night, God sent His angel through the camp of the Assyrians and destroyed 185,000 enemy soldiers. God's agents were on duty as usual.

But what about in modern times? Is God still fighting for Israel? A thundering affirmative! Tremendously so! Michael and his angels are busy.

Our good friend Rev. Hilton Sutton, who served in the Air Force during World War II, has given some exciting testimonies concerning Michael's divine intervention in behalf of Israel during that war. Israel has been through difficult times and survived, but nothing more heinous than the holocaust in which six million Jews were put to death by Adolph Hitler. Hitler's intent was to destroy every Jew, and probably would have succeeded except for God's intervention with His angels.

World War II effectively began in September of 1939 when Hitler invaded Poland. Within a few days Poland collapsed. After leaving Poland in flames, the vast armies of Germany moved west.

All the world looked on in wonder. And the armies of heaven under Michael did more than observe. Everyone thought that France, with the largest standing army of any nation in the world, six million soldiers, would hold out against Hitler. But, in ten short months, Germany had marched across Europe, absolutely demoralizing the allied armies, breaking their military back.

It was a discouraged, depressed, and tattered Allied army that stood on the banks of the English Channel at Dunkirk, France, waiting for the British to come across the channel in anything that would float and bring back at least one more survivor. It was a miracle of God the English were able to evacuate as many troops as they did. But this defeat meant the last of much of the equipment of the Allied armies, their equipment being either left behind for the Germans or totally destroyed in battle. England became the last stronghold of freedom for that part of the world.

It looked to all the world that Hitler had succeeded.

Hitler was an unusual man, to say the least. I heard his recorded voice once during a speech class in college. It was as if Satan himself spoke through Hitler. He had the uncanny, almost supernatural ability to excite and stir men to action. Hitler was not particularly brilliant, but he had the satanic ability to control men and surround himself with brilliant and powerful men.

Hitler used his satanic ability to develop the most powerful army the world had ever known. His master plan and determined goal was total world control, with himself as dictator. He intended to create a superior race of people and had a satanic desire to eliminate the Jewish people from off the face of the earth.

Michael had to do something and fast. Only the small nation of England remained to stop Hitler's drive.

The Allied troops had no sooner safely reached British soil from France when Hitler mysteriously called a surprise meeting of his staff of generals made up of the military geniuses of the world. Hitler asked his staff of generals to reach a decision as to whether to invade England or to wait for a more opportune time. It was almost insane. When could there have possibly been a better time? Hitler had the distraught Allied army in his hip pocket!

Even considering a stiff fight from the British Isles, Hitler could have won within a matter of months. There really wasn't a decision to make. But a strange general, not a German, a man not known to Hitler's staff, showed up at the meeting. This strange general persuaded Hitler and his staff to not invade England, but to wait until the German army was stronger, when victory was assured. It was decided the German army would invade Russia rather than England.

Had Hitler made the decision to take England, even though it might have required a full year of fighting to do so, and then moved eastward to invade Russia, the outcome of World War II would have been far different. Hitler would have taken all the world, with the exception of the western hemisphere. And the United States could not have held up forever against that fearsome force.

Hitler and his staff of military geniuses listened to the strange visiting general and invaded Russia instead of England. That decision was Germany's Waterloo.

General Rommel, the German "desert fox," had General Montgomery of England and his forces on the run in North Africa. In fact, General Rommel had won every major military encounter and English morale was extremely low. General Rommel had devised a plan which he felt certain would once and for all break Montgomery's military back.

Rommel's troops were poised like a coiled rattlesnake and ready to strike the tiring British army. But before Rommel could strike, Hitler again called a mysterious surprise meeting of his staff of generals. Again, the strange visiting general appeared at the meeting. This time the visiting general convinced them to recall Rommel to Germany and to replace him in North Africa with a general totally unprepared for attack.

The new general devised his own strategy against Montgomery. But this gave the British field marshal time to rally his forces and launch a counterattack, which resulted in a major victory for England. The morale of the British troops zoomed upward. The tide of battle turned in North Africa.

It was going bad for the Germans on the eastern front, as well. The Americans had gotten into the war and the Germans were in retreat.

Again, Hitler called a staff meeting to make a major decision, whether to assembly-line-produce jet aircraft, or to continue hurling bombs at Britain. The strange general was in attendance again and overwhelmingly convinced Hitler and his staff not to take the time to set up assembly line production of jet aircraft.

By the time the Germans realized their mistake in not mass-producing jet planes, the United States had gained total air supremacy and was able to raze almost all German industry through continued air strikes.

Who in the world was this strange visiting general who continued to influence Hitler and his brilliant staff? Nobody in the world could have pulled off such a daring feat. It was none other than Michael, Chief of Staff of the Armies of Heaven.

WOW! That's hard to believe. But wait a minute. It is often recorded in the Old Testament where God sent a tumult through the enemies of Israel and put them in such confusion they defeated themselves. God sent His angels to stir up the camp of the enemy to such a degree they actually defeated themselves. There are numerous biblical records of such events. If God did it then, couldn't He do it in our time?

The Bible says Michael was given a special assignment in behalf of Israel. Michael began his special assignment during the 1930s and he is continuing it to this very hour. At the end of World War II, Israel was delivered, as was prophesied in Daniel 2. The Israelis were delivered and returned to their own land where they are today.

Only an influence from God could have caused the powerful German armies not to pursue and destroy the English, French, and other armies across the narrow English Channel. Only God could have caused the Germans to withdraw General Rommel from a sure victory against North Africa. And only divine intervention prevented the Germans from mass-producing jet aircraft when they had every capability of doing it and of attaining world air supremacy and thus winning World War II.

Had they won, all Jews would have been put to death. Satan would have ruled the world through Hitler. But it was not time. God still had much work for the Christians to do. Many people were praying. God sent Michael to turn the tide of the war. God's Word could not fail. The Jews had to be preserved.

After the war many Jews came out of hiding. And as the prophet Zephaniah says in chapter 2, the Jews went home. Not a home without trouble, but for the first time in thousands of years, a home.

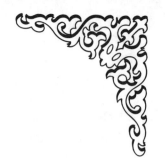

Chapter 26

War Beyond the Stars

Way back in the eons of time there was a great war in the heavens, far beyond the star systems, far beyond all galaxies. It was a war beyond the realm of the imagination of even the most imaginative science fiction writers. It was a war of wars. A war so terrible that all the universe was shaken.

The great war was waged between super creatures traveling with the speed of thought. Creatures with the ability to travel throughout the vast space of the universe in a shorter time than it takes to think of the name of their destination.

The great war started when a space creature of awesome power and aesthetic beauty became envious of God, his Creator. At that time all the angelic creatures served God because they desired to do so. They had freedom of choice, or a will to choose.

One of these high-ranking angelic beings said in his heart, "I will exalt myself above the most high God. I will move my throne above the stars."

This great angelic creature was persuasive and convincing and was able to gather around him one-third of all the angelic space creatures who ruled with God over the universe. The angelic creatures in rebellion rallied around the person of Lucifer, the bright star of the universe. They made plans for the great war in which they desired to usurp control of the universe from God Almighty, their Creator.

Space vehicles known as fiery chariots were launched into space. The great war raged. Planets and stars throughout the universe were shaken as Lucifer and one-third of all the angels in heaven were defeated and cast down from the heavens.

Jesus said of this great war, years later when he was on earth living as a man, "I beheld Satan as lightning fall from the heavens." Jesus was there with the Father when the great war was fought.

Lucifer, the bright star of heaven, once reigned over the earth. The earth was in all probability the place of his throne. For he said he would move his throne above the clouds and beyond the stars.

Lucifer's rebellion is described in Ezekiel 28:13-19 and in Isaiah 14:12-17. God and His angels won the war, but the battles rage on even today.

Since the two-thirds of all the angels remaining with God had made an eternal decision to remain loyal to God's throne, they would never again be faced with such terrible temptation. After the war, God had angelic creatures surrounding Him who worshipped and served Him because they desired to do so.

Thus, it has always been the nature of God to desire companionship from creatures who desire His companionship.

God, being the Father of the universe and the Creator of all things, could easily create any number of creatures to worship Him. But true companionship is an entirely different matter. It comes only from those giving fellowship because they desire to do so, not because they are forced or are created to give companionship.

So, many years after the great war in space, as man measures time, it entered the heart of God to create a creature like himself, one in His own image, with abilities very near those of His own. A creature that could some day rule and reign the universe with Him.

What could be a more suitable home for this new creature than planet Earth, where the now dethroned Lucifer once reigned? And also there was a dispute still to be settled. Lucifer had contended that created creatures would not worship God out of free will and that he, Lucifer, could persuade God's creatures to leave God and worship him.

This contention had to be answered by a just God. Otherwise, God could be considered unjust in punishing Lucifer for his rebellion. Lucifer must be given opportunity to tempt God's created creatures into worshiping him rather than God, their Creator.

So on earth God created a man in His own image, a creature with awesome power to reign over earth. Of course, man was given a woman to be his companion.

Man was created with a will, or the ability to choose. Lucifer was given the opportunity to prove his point and succeeded in persuading the woman to disobey God and to follow Lucifer. The man followed the woman, not because he was beguiled by Lucifer, but because he desired the companionship of the woman more than that of God, his Creator. The sin of the man was far worse than that of the woman.

Because of man's great and terrible sin against God, the whole earth was thrown out of order. Lucifer gained control of the planet Earth and became known as the god of this world.

Lucifer, or Satan, became man's eternal enemy. Thousands of years later, God sent His own Son, Jesus, in the form of a man to successfully overcome the power of Satan and to take from him the power and authority held by Adam, the first man. Jesus became known as the second Adam. The successful Adam. Jesus proved that it was possible for a human, a man created in the image of God, to overcome every temptation of Satan and remain true to God. Jesus restored the human race to its rightful place of authority and power under God.

The Bible tells of another war at the end of this age. A war in all probability even more terrible than the first war. This is the final space war. A war in which the last of Satan's power will be taken from him. Again, it is a war between super creatures in outer space.

The super war is described in Revelation 122:7-9. "And there was war in heaven: Michael and his angels fought against the dragon [Satan]; and the dragon fought and his angels, and prevailed not; neither was their place found any more in heaven. And the great dragon was cast out, that old serpent, called the Devil, and Satan, which deceiveth the whole world: he was cast out into the earth, and his angels were cast out with him."

In that terrible war will be launched the super vehicles known as the chariots of God. These vehicles are more fully described in Zechariah 6; Isaiah 66:15; Psalm 68:17 and 104:3; and Habakkuk 3:8.

It is interesting to note that whenever there has been a major confrontation between Israel and her Arab cousins, there has always been an accompanying rash of UFOs. This is a matter of record. There were many sightings of UFOs in 1947, the War of Independence; again in 1956, the war with Egypt in the Sinai Peninsula; 1967, the year of the Six-Day War; and finally in 1973, the Yom Kippur War. Every major conflict against Israel had been accompanied by a deluge of UFOs.

These UFOs are described accurately in Ezekiel 1. Here we learn that the heavenly chariots travel as a flash of lightning. The United States Air Force over the years has accumulated information on the movement and description of UFOs which closely fits the description given in Ezekiel.

Air force jets have chased UFOs which apparently moved with almost infinite speed and unlimited mobility. The UFOs can make 90-degree turns while flying at top speed. These characteristics also match those given by Ezekiel. The air force has photographed UFOs with rings or portholes all the way around the mysterious space ship. Ezekiel also describes this.

In Ezekiel 10, the strange creatures are described as an order of cherubims. These are apparently warrior creatures of the heavenly armies under the control of Michael.

Apparently, Satan and his angels also have fiery chariots available to them. There have been many sightings of a different type of UFO each time the first kind appears. The second type of UFO has been described as giving off a pulsating light, not a constant bright light as emitted by the first type. And their movement has been described as erratic.

Fear and confusion have always been accompanied by close encounters with the second type of UFO. In 1973, the year of the Israeli Yom Kippur War, two men in Mississippi underwent a terrible encounter with a demonic UFO. The traumatic experiences described by these men could have been caused by nothing less than Satan's angels.

Could it not be that these UFOs are actually sightings of the supernatural space vehicles engaged in terrible battle over the nation Israel? The description fits perfectly.

The important thing is that the conflict between good and evil angels still rages, and will continue to do so until that last great war described in Revelation 12. Super space creatures contend for the control of nations. This is evident from Daniel 10:10-14:

> And, behold, an hand touched me, which set me upon my knees, and upon the palms of my hands. And he said unto me, O Daniel, a man greatly beloved, understand the words that I speak unto thee, and stand upright: for unto thee am I now sent. And when he had spoken this word unto me, I stood trembling. Then said he unto me, Fear not, Daniel: for from the first day that thou didst set thine heart to understand, and to chasten thyself before thy God, thy words were heard, and I am come for thy words. But the prince of the kingdom of Persia withstood me one and twenty days: but, lo, Michael, one of the chief princes, came to help me; and I remained there with the kings of Persia. Now I am come to make thee understand what shall befall thy people in the latter days: for yet the vision is for many days.

And the angel continues his story in Daniel 10:20-21:

> Then said he, Knowest thou wherefore I come unto thee? and now will I return to fight with the prince of Persia: and when I am gone forth, lo, the prince of Grecia shall come. But I will shew thee that which is noted in the scripture of truth: and there is none that holdeth with me in these things, but Michael your prince.

Here is recorded an account of satanic creatures who rule over specific

nations actually attacking an angelic creature sent by God to Daniel. This reveals there is a constant conflict between super creatures in outer space, and sometimes answers to prayers may be delayed because of the struggle.

It also reveals the necessity for prayer, and especially persistent prayer for our nation and for those in office in our government.

Evil, satanic space creatures desire to rule and control our nation. But the believer has the authority through the name of Jesus Christ to call for God's angels to form a garrison about our nation, about the president, every member of Congress, and every member of the Supreme Court. Prayer and supplication should be made every day for the leaders of our great nation.

The apostle Paul reveals the intricate organization of Satan's forces in Ephesians 6:12;NAS: "For our struggle is not against flesh and blood, but against the rulers, against the powers, against the world forces of this darkness, against the spiritual [superhuman] forces of wickedness in the heavenly places."

This organization of Satan is the vast force behind organized crime, drug traffic, and the sinister plot by the Satan worshipers to control the world. This is the organization giving to men the knowledge and wisdom to promote Communism around the world.

These satanic space creatures cause accidents, disasters, storms, earthquakes, and anything else that destroys or kills. For to kill and destroy is the purpose of Satan. Jesus came that we might have abundant life.

Jesus once rebuked a storm caused by Satan. The modern day believer can do the same thing Jesus did. For Jesus said, "Behold, I give you power over all the power of the enemy" (Luke 10:19).

When the believer prays in the name of Jesus, there is dispatched from the Father's throne angelic space creatures to bring about the answer to the prayer. And, if like Daniel of old, reinforcements become necessary to answer the prayer, then additional forces will be immediately dispatched. There are twice as many good angels as evil angels. God has an army of an estimated one hundred trillion angels.

God's angels are highly organized. Each one has ability and a personality of his own. Each angel has specific duties and sufficient wisdom and knowledge to execute those duties.

Apparently this is not true of Satan and his angels. For it is known that Satan played right into God's plan for his defeat when he put Jesus Christ on the cross and took a righteous man, a man completely without sin, into hell.

Satan, by taking Jesus into hell, broke a rule of the universe which had been established from the beginning, right after the great war beyond the stars. Satan lost his power and authority when he took Jesus, a perfect man.

Satan lost all authority over the believer. He has absolutely no authority except as allowed by God. What Satan does to the believer he does because of the believer's ignorance of Satan's defeat by Jesus.

It is apparent by observing satanic activity in organized crime, in his work among the nations, or in his spread of Communism, that the evil angels often become confused and turn against themselves. For example, there are many instances in the wars against Israel where the enemy became confused and destroyed their own troops and installations.

The important thing is that the believer has the "greater One abiding within." There is also available angel power through Christ, far superior to the forces of Satan.

There will be a great war in heaven when Michael and his angels completely defeat Satan and his angels, and Satan will no longer have access to the heavens to accuse the believer. Satan will be bound in the depths of hell.

Until that time the conflict rages through space, invisible warriors moving with the speed of thought carrying out the orders of their leaders. Many of these creatures are on their way with messages to the international leaders of the Communist countries, to the international league of Satan worshipers who so sinisterly plan world rule, or even to leaders of our government who may elect to use their office to further plans of such sinister groups.

But, even as Daniel of old received some of his wisdom and knowledge from an angel, so can the believer request that God send angels to bring wisdom, knowledge, and protection to the leaders of our nation. The believer does not have to yield to Satan's plans for this nation.

By rising up in prayer, the believer can do something about gasoline shortages, about inflation, about planned strikes to immobilize shipments and traffic. Yes, the believer can do something to strengthen this great nation so vital to the ministry of the gospel around the world in these closing hours of this age.

There is vast angel power available to knock down the forces of hell that come against the work of God. It is time to put away weak and watered-down religious traditions that have plagued believers for years. In our time God is raising up true believers, men and woman who are taking the time to read the contract and find for themselves what God gave them through Jesus Christ. You can and should be one of these informed ones.

Please direct inquiries to:

Joel and Jane French
P.O. Box 1452
Humble, TX 77347

About the Authors

Joel and Jane French are a husband and wife writing team. When not research-ing and writing, Joel is a management consultant and college professor and Jane teaches the fifth grade.